12-76

from Lynne + Damion X-mas #76

from Lynne + Damion X-mas #76

Paul W. Hendrickson

A CENTURY OF GUNS.

Drawn by William Marlow Esq.r F.S.A.   Published as the Act directs Nov.r 1st 1795 by John Curtis Twickenham Middlesex.   Engraved by Tho.s Prond of the late Ingenious M.r Woollett
& to be had of M.r March   Stationer Ludgate Hill

FISH STREET HILL, LONDON, 1795.

A CENTURY OF GUNS:

A SKETCH OF THE LEADING TYPES OF SPORTING AND MILITARY SMALL ARMS,

WITH OVER 150 ILLUSTRATIONS OF GUNS AND RIFLES.

———————

"UNTO THE GUYLE OF ALL ARTILLERY,
CROSS-BOWS, HAND-GUNS, AND OF ARCHERY."

Dedication of the Artillery Garden, London, 1622.
From Stow's Survey of London, Ed. 1633.

BY H. J. BLANCH

EP PUBLISHING LIMITED
1976

Republished 1976 by
EP Publishing Limited
East Ardsley, Wakefield
West Yorkshire, England

First published 1909 by John Blanch & Son

British Library Cataloguing in Publication Data
Blanch, H. J.
    A century of guns.
    Index.
    ISBN 0-7158-1156-8
    1. Title
    683' .4'09034   TS533
    Firearms-History-Early works

ISBN 0 7158 1156 8

Please address all enquiries to EP Publishing Limited
(address as above)

Printed in Great Britain by
The Scolar Press Limited, Ilkley, West Yorkshire

33 *Statute of Henry VIII.*

❧ ❧ ❧

§ " *Provided alway, and be it enacted, &c., that it shall be lawful, from henceforth, to all gentlemen yeomen, and serving-men of every lord, spiritual and temporal, and of all knights, esquires, and gentlemen, and to all the inhabitants of cities, boroughs, and market towns, of this Realm of England, to shoot with any hand-gun, demihake, or hagbut, at any butt or bank of earth, only in places convenient for the same; so that every such hand-gun, &c., be of the several lengths aforesaid, and not under. And that it shall be lawful, to every of the said lord and lords, knights, esquires, and gentlemen, and the inhabitants of every city, borough and market town, to have and keep in every of their houses such hand-gun or hand-guns, of the length of one whole yard, &c., and not under, to the intent to use and shoot in the same, at a butt or bank of earth only, as is above said, whereby they and every of them, by the exercise thereof, in form above said, may the better aid and assist to the defence of this realm, when need shall require, &c.*"

GUNSMITHS IN THE LONDON DIRECTORY, 1812.

BAKER, EZEKIEL, 24, Whitechapel Road.

BARNETT, THOMAS, 134, Minories.

BARTON, JOHN, 14, Haymarket.

BECKWITH, W., 58, Skinner Street, Snow Hill.

BLAKE, ANN, 95, Wapping Old Stairs.

BLANCH, JOHN, 39, Fish Street Hill.

BOND, P., 45, Cornhill

BOND, WILLIAM, 59, Lombard Street.

BRANDER & POTTS, 70, Minories.

BRUNN, S., 56, Charing Cross.

EGG, DURS, 132, Strand.

FISHER, C. B., 39, Greek Street, Soho.

FORSYTH & CO., Patent Gunmakers, 10, Piccadilly.

FULLERD, WILLIAM (Barrelmaker), 57, Compton Street, Clerkenwell.

GILL, THOMAS, 83, St. James' Street.

GRIERSON, C., 10, New Bond Street (to His Majesty).

GULLEY, JOSEPH, 254, Oxford Street.

HENSON, THOMAS, 34, Piccadilly.

JOHNSTON, RICHARD, 68, St. James' Street.

LEIGH, JAMES, 10, George Street, Tower Hill.

MANTON, JOHN (Patent Gunmaker to their Royal Highnesses the Prince of Wales and Duke of York), 6, Dover Street, Piccadilly.

MANTON, JOSEPH (Patentee for the Elevation and Breeching of Guns and Hammers of Locks, also Patentee for Chronometers going in Vacuo), 27, Davies Street, Berkeley Square.

MARWOOD, WILLIAM, 52, Mansell Street.

MORTIMER, JACKSON & SON, 21, St. James' Street.

MORTIMER, THOMAS & SON, 44, Ludgate Hill.

MORTIMER, H. W., jun., 89, Fleet Street (to His Majesty).

NOCK, SAMUEL, 180, Fleet Street (to His Majesty).

PARKER, WILLIAM, 233, High Holborn.

PEAKE, JOHN, 38, Leman Street, Goodman's Fields.

PRITCHETT, S., 37, Chambers Street, Goodman's Fields.

REA, JOHN & SON, 91, Minories.

RICHARDS, JOHN, 55, Strand.

RIDLEY, T., 24, Chambers Street, Goodman's Fields.

RIDLEY, W., 21, Chambers Street, Goodman's Fields.

SHERWOOD, JOHN, 67, Upper East Smithfield.

SMITH, WILLIAM, 2, New Lisle Street, Leicester Square.

STANDENMAYER, S. H., 35, Cockspur Street (to H.R.H. Duke of York).

TATHAM & EGG, 37, Charing Cross.

THOMPSON, JAMES, 18, Swan Street, Minories.

UTTING, JOHN, 265, Borough.

WILKINSON, JAMES, 17, Ludgate Hill (to His Majesty).

WILLSON, ALEXANDER, 3, Sherrard Street, Golden Square.

WILSON, ALEXANDER, 14, Tichborne Street, Piccadilly.

WILSON, WILLIAM, 154, Minories.

WRIGHT, ROBERT, 44, Great Prescott Street.

YEOMANS, J., 40, Chambers Street, Goodman's Fields.

YORK, CHARLES, 151, Grub Street.

TOWER VOLUNTEER, 1802.

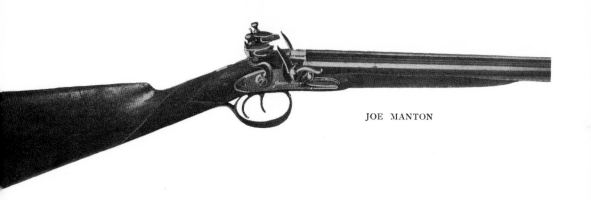

JOE MANTON

PREFACE.

THE century which has just elapsed since John Blanch started as a gunsmith, at 39, Fish Street Hill, which then led down on to Old London Bridge, close to the Monument, has witnessed the development of the Magazine Rifle by easy stages from the Flint Lock "Brown Bess" Musket, and the Hammerless Ejector Double Gun from the Flint Lock Double Muzzleloader of "Joe Manton." As a lad, John Blanch was apprenticed to the well-known gunsmith, Jackson Mortimer, of 21, St. James's Street, and like the proverbial good apprentice, he married his master's daughter.

There were three firms of the name of Mortimer, of which the senior was Harvey Walklate Mortimer, who had a shop in Fleet Street in 1780, at the time of the Lord George Gordon Riots, when most of the other gunsmiths sent their goods to the Tower of London for safe keeping; but he declined to do so, and was rewarded by disposing of his stock at high prices.

John Blanch served for three years with John Manton, elder brother, or half-brother of "Joe," and the leading gunsmith of the time, although, later on, the younger brother became the more

ix.

famous; and having learnt the craft of gunsmithery under two such competent instructors, started for himself in the city in 1809.

About 1826, John Blanch removed his business, when new London Bridge was building, to 29, Gracechurch Street, where it is still carried on. In 1836 his eldest son went out to Tasmania, as a gunsmith. He had for a time been in business at Hull, where he had carried out experiments on the sands with a line throwing gun of his own construction. The developments then beginning round Melbourne (as it is now called) induced him to move there in 1837 or 1838, and he had only been there about a year when he was killed by an explosion of gunpowder at his own store in Market Square. In those days gunpowder was packed loose in barrels and weighed out to purchasers to fill their flasks. In 1848, John Blanch took his third son, William, into partnership, and the title of the firm was altered to John Blanch and Son. Of the gunsmiths' names appearing in the Post Office London Directory for 1812, only three still appear in the same category—Barnett, Blanch, and Wilkinson.

Henry Wilkinson, who published a book in 1841 on "Engines of War," was grandson of Henry Nock, who invented the concave breech plug in 1787, so long known as the "Patent Breech"; he also introduced the short flat piece on the top of the barrel at the breech end, which is still known as the "Nock Form," and survives in the Martini and other rifles. Although lighter and neater than an octagonal breech end, it gives an excellent grip for clamps when unscrewing the breech plug or action from barrel. H. Nock and D. Egg made some of the most elegant models of duelling pistols with hair triggers, which were not too heavy to use as holster pistols when

PREFACE.

travelling; these had the wood of the stock right up to the muzzle. Some of the later duelling pistols had very heavy octagonal barrels with a rib underneath, and the stock only half way up, which were too heavy for anything but the "affair of honour"

As there were no railways or police in those days, when travelling more than a few miles, either on horseback, by post chaise, or coach, it was usual to go armed, and so Blunderbusses and Pistols, Horse Pistols for holsters, Sash Pistols with a long hook for the belt or sash, and Pocket Pistols for the big side pockets of the coat, were a regular article of home demand; and duelling with pistols was by no means obsolete, and was not finally suppressed in the Army until 1844.

In arranging the series of illustrations in the following pages, I am indebted to the following gentlemen for the loan of valuable pieces from their collections.

The three fine old Flint Lock Pistols in group 17 are from the collection of H. J. Jackson, Esq., Walpole, Chislehurst, Kent. The Sam Smith Double Flint Lock Gun (Samuel and Charles Smith, successors to William Smith, 2, New Lisle Street, Leicester Square, London), and the original Forsyth Detonator, both in group 1, and several other double guns, also the Forsyth Detonator Pistols in group 2, are from the collection of P. E. Schweder, Esq., Courtlands, Goring, Sussex. The larger proportion of the early breechloading military rifles and carbines are from the very complete collection formed by H. H. Harrod, Esq., The Red House, Bishopsdown, Tunbridge Wells. The breechloading Flint Lock Rifle, by Durs Egg, was for many years in the Rotunda at Woolwich, and was lent by Thomas B. Winser, Esq., of 81, Shooter's Hill Road, Blackheath,

PREFACE.

Kent, who was the original founder of the International Rifle Match so well known as the Elcho Shield, a trophy given by Lord Elcho (now Earl Wemyss) in 1862, and annually competed for ever since by teams of eight a side from England, Scotland, Wales and Ireland.

The Ferguson breechloading Flint Lock Rifle was lent by J. H. White, Esq., Springfield, Chelmsford, Essex.

I have also to express my thanks to my friend, Mr. R. H. Angier for the carefully compiled Tables of Particulars of Modern Rifles, and the drawings of Military Rifle Cartridges.

H. J. BLANCH.

April, 1909.

DUELLING PISTOL	..	..	H. NOCK.
DUELLING PISTOL	..	..	D. EGG.
DUELLING PISTOL	..	..	W. BECKWITH.
HOLSTER PISTOL	..	..	J. BLANCH.

CONTENTS.

OLD STAGE CARRIAGE, SHEWING "GUARD" ARMED WITH A BLUNDERBUSS.

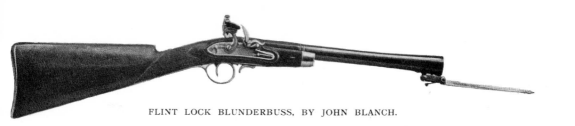

FLINT LOCK BLUNDERBUSS, BY JOHN BLANCH.

A CENTURY OF GUNS.

CHAPTER I.

FLINT LOCK PERIOD. VOLUNTEERS. MUSKETS AND RIFLES.

A CENTURY ago London was the centre of the gun trade of this country, and the workers were numerous, especially about the Minories and Goodman's Fields near the Tower, where they had been established since Queen Elizabeth's days. The name of the Minories referred to a Convent which stood here from 1293, until it was surrendered to Henry VIII. in 1539, as Stow tells us in his "Survey of London," 1598, and then he adds :—

"In place of this house of nuns is now built divers fair and large storehouses for armour and habiliments of war with divers workhouses *(sic)* serving to the same purpose."

"Neere adjoyning to this Abby, on the South side thereof, was sometime a Farme belonging to the said Nunrie, at the which Farme, I myselfe (in my youth) have fetched many a halfe-penny worth of milke, and never had lesse than three ale pintes for a

B

halfe-penny in the summer, nor lesse than one ale quart for a halfe-penny in the winter, alwaies hot from the kine, as the same was milked and strained. One Trolop and afterwards Goodman, were the Farmers there, and had thirty or forty kine to the paile. Goodman's son being heire to his father's purchase, let out the ground, first for grazing of horses, and then for Garden plots, and lived like a Gentleman thereby."

Close by was the Proof House, established by Charter of Charles I., in 1637, in whose time old Pepys lived in Seething Lane, and doubtless it was from a neighbouring shop that he fetched Truelocke, the gunsmith, whom he mentions under date :—

"March 29, 1667, To the Bull-Head Taverne, whither was brought my French gun : and one Truelocke, the famous gunsmith, that is a mighty ingenious man, did take my gun in pieces, and made me understand the secrets thereof ; and upon the whole I do find it a very good piece of work, and truly wrought ; but for certain not a thing to be used much with safety ; and he do find that this very gun was never yet shot off."

But to return to the early nineteenth century, and the time of the great war with Napoleon. In those days there was no Government Small Arms Factory, and the gunsmiths who took up various lines of the trade sent in consignments to be viewed and accepted at the Tower. An old workman of ours used to relate an incident that his father was a witness to. Having delivered some work at the Tower he saw another workman delivering bayonets, one of which was rejected by the viewer as being under size, much to the discomfiture of the man, whose money would be short, and who, in order to relieve his feelings, as he was passing out, shouted—"What ! That not strong enough to kill a Frenchman?" and then with a powerful stroke, struck it right through the door, in which he left it sticking, and swaggered away.

Two things, which we are apt to connect with mid-Victorian times, had their origins even before these days—Rifles and the Volunteers. Although the Volunteers were not all armed with Rifles, some of them were, such as the Duke of Cumberland's Sharpshooters, 1803; Dukinfield Independent Riflemen, 1804; Manchester Rifle Regiment, 1804; Rutland Legion Riflemen, 1796; Sutton's (Captain) Rifle Company, 1805; and the Cambridge University Rifles. They were very resplendent as to uniform, the Inns of Court Volunteers, or "Devil's Own" as they were called even in those days, sporting a yellow jacket and a fearsome busby with white breeches and long black cloth gaiters—the latter much affected by the military of the Georgian period. On one occasion, this corps or association as they were sometimes called in the old books was reviewed by the Earl of Harrington, and after saluting the commander he said: "This is the Law Association, Sir?" "Yes, my Lord;" to which the Earl rejoined: "I do not find anyone that speaks a word; I never saw lawyers so silent." "We have no pay, my Lord," replied Colonel Erskine. The Bridge Ward Volunteers had red jackets, a helmet with black plume, blue smalls, and short black cloth gaiters.

The admirable coloured prints, by Rowlandson, of the Loyal Volunteers of the time, show a wonderful fancy and variety in the military costume of the period. The Tower Volunteers, of which we have an illustration, had red jackets, and were evidently armed with the musket. In 1804, there were 350,000 Volunteers, of which

46,000 were Metropolitan : they were disbanded in 1814. In 1803 Napoleon, who was still First Consul, had 114,554 troops at Boulogne and 2,000 ships and boats. The following three extracts are from "Napoleon and the Invasion of England," by Messrs. Wheeler and Broadley (John Lane), 1908 :—

"The Association for Promoting the Defence of the Firth of Forth and Scotland in General, was started in 1803, and in their first report it is stated—'many of the companies in this district have by practice acquired so great a degree of proficiency, that in their exercise every fifth or sixth shot is made to take place in a target of three feet diameter at the distance of about 100 yards. This with the common battalion firelock, is a high degree of precision ; and if accuracy on a proportionate scale may be expected from them in battle, the efficiency of the military defence of the country will thereby, it is evident, be greatly augmented.'"

"In *The Times* of the 6th August, 1803, a writer sums up the progress of the volunteer movement as follows :—'Eleven weeks are barely passed since the declaration of war, and we defy any man living to mention a period when half so much was ever effected in the same space of time, for the defence of the country. 1st.—A naval force such as Great Britain never had before, has been completely equipped, manned, and in readiness to meet the enemy. 2nd.—The regular military force of the kingdom has been put on the most respectable footing. 3rd.—The militia has been called forth, and encamped with the regular forces. 4th.—The supplementary militia has been embodied, and even encamped. 5th.—An army of reserve of 50,000 men has been already added to this force, and is now in great forwardness. 6th.—A measure has been adopted for calling out and arming the whole mass of the people, in case of emergency ; and we are confident that our information is correct when we say that at this moment there are nearly 300,000 men enrolled in different Volunteer, Yeomanry, and Cavalry Corps, of whom at least a third may be considered as already disciplined and accoutred.'"

· " Lord Chatham, Master General of the Ordnance, writing to Wilberforce, September 2nd, 1803, states that after the restoration of peace (Amiens 1802) he endeavoured to replenish the supply of 'the old Tower musquet, which our troops used to have,' and of an improved pattern, but admits that owing to the 'naked state of our arsenals' an inferior weapon had to be manufactured. No sooner had he 'nearly surmounted' this difficulty than 'this sudden and unprecedented demand for arms took place.' But he is forced to admit a still more humiliating fact : ' Had it not been with a view to improvement, and intending gradually to dispose of those of inferior quality through the medium of the India Company, we should not have been, previous to the war breaking out, carrying on any manufacture of arms, our arsenals being overflowing, calculating on the extended scale the Department has ever been called upon to furnish. I have, however, in consequence of the extraordinary calls of the present crisis, determined to use every effort to meet it, and directions have been given to the Board of Ordnance to revert to the same arm as was made last war, and to manufacture to the utmost possible extent the musquets of the India pattern. You will easily believe I must have felt some reluctance in being obliged to take this step after all the pains I have bestowed, but I hope I have judged for the best. I have great satisfaction in thinking that the stock of arms we possess will enable us in the first instance to arm to a considerable extent perhaps all that is really useful, and as arms come in, which with the exertions of the manufacturers they will do quickly, and with the aid of what we expect from abroad, the remainder will be provided before long. We have already one hundred thousand pikes, and can

AFTER JAMES GILLRAY.
ADDINGTON, PRIME MINISTER, 1801—4 AND NAPOLEON.

increase them rapidly, but in general there is an indisposition to take them. I should like much to talk over with you not only the subject of arms, but the whole question of volunteering, which I contemplate as a most serious one.'" *Private Papers of William Wilberforce.*

The London Volunteers were raised under an Act of 1661, confirming previous like privileges, which were again confirmed by George I., George II., and George III.

Act of 13 and 14, Charles II., c. 3, section 27 :—"Provided always, and be it enacted by the authority aforesaid, that His Majesty's lieutenants that are or shall be commissioned for the Militia of the City of London, may and shall continue to list and levy the Trained Bands and Auxiliaries of the said City, ... from time to time, to levy and call together, receive and entertain, all and singular our subjects, both volunteers and others."

Lord Clarendon, speaking of the Battle of Newbury, 1644, says :—" The London Trained Bands and Auxiliary Regiments (of whose inexperience of danger, beyond the easy practice of their postures in the Artillery garden, men had till then too cheap an estimation) behaved themselves to wonder ; and were, in truth, the preservation of that army that day. For they stood as a bulwark and rampire to defend the rest ; and, when their wings of horse were scattered and dispersed, kept their ground so steadily, that, though Prince Rupert himself led up the choice horse to charge them, and endured their storm of small shot, he could make no impression upon their stand of pikes, but was forced to wheel about : of so sovereign benefit and use is that readiness, order, and dexterity, in the use of their arms, which hath been so much neglected."—Book 7, pg. 268, folio ed. 1707.

The Flint Lock Musket, the principal weapon in use in the early nineteenth century, was known as the "Brown Bess" (Group 3, Fig. 11), the name being connected with the colour of the barrel ; the Match Lock Musket, which it superseded about 1700, apparently having a bright metal barrel.   It was employed in all the campaigns of Marlborough and Wellington, and fired a round ball of about fourteen to the pound.

Colonel Hanger, 1814, says :—"A soldier's musket, if not exceedingly ill-bored (as many are), will strike the figure of a man at 80 yards ; it may even at a hundred ; but a soldier must be very unfortunate indeed who shall be wounded by a common musket at 150 yards, provided his antagonist aims at him ; and, as to firing at a man at 200 yards with a common musket, you may just as well fire at the moon and have the same hopes of hitting your object.   I do maintain and will prove, whenever called on, that no man was ever killed at 200 yards, by a common soldier's musket, by the person who aimed at him."

" In 1834, the Rev. Mr. Forsyth (the inventor of the percussion system) induced the Government to try a number of experiments, in order to test the value of his invention as compared with the old flint lock, and the result of these experiments was as follows :—Six thousand rounds were fired from a flint lock musket and a percussion musket, and the experiments were conducted in all weathers, six of each kind of arm being used.   The results proved exceedingly favourable to the percussion principle, for out of 6,000 rounds from the flint lock there were 922 miss-fires, being 1 in 6½, whereas in the percussion musket there were only 36 misses in 6,000 rounds, or 1 in 166.   The flint musket scored 3,680 hits ; the percussion, 4,047.   To fire 100 rounds the flint required 32 min. 31 sec., and the percussion, 30 min. 24 sec."

"About 1841, the Royal Engineers were employed to ascertain and define the real properties or capabilities of the genuine old

GROUP I.

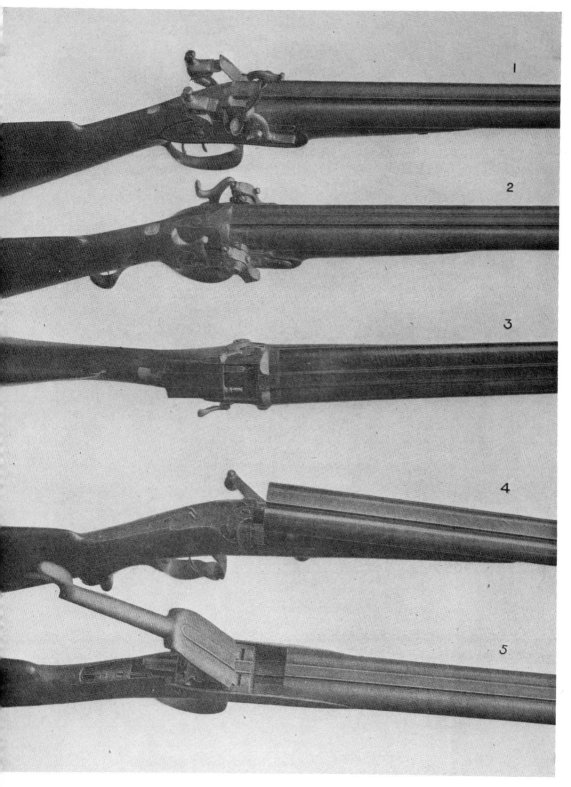

INT LOCK DOUBLE GUN, BY SAMUEL AND CHARLES SMITH, LONDON
(ABOUT 1809).
RSYTH DETONATOR DOUBLE GUN, WITH MAGAZINE PRIMERS (1807).
FORMERLY IN THE POSSESSION OF THE LATE DUKE OF CAMBRIDGE.

3. CENTRAL FIRE MUZZLELOADING DOUBLE GUN, CHARLES JONES'S
PATENT (1833). THE CAPS WERE PLACED ON THE NOSE OF THE
HAMMERS AND HAD THE DETONATING COMPOSITION OUTSIDE ON
THE CROWN OF THE CAP.
4. DOUBLE NEEDLE-GUN. C. F. BEDDIES, BRUNSWICK (1850-60).

5. CHATAUVILLAR-MONTIGNY, BRUSSELS (1849). NEEDLE-FIRE.

'service musket,' which had carried the British soldier through so many fights, and which high military authorities most tenaciously endeavoured to preserve. So a body of officers went to work at Chatham, with all the appliances necessary for the precise establishment of the facts, and this is what they found :—They discovered that as to the distance a regulation musket would carry, nothing more certain could be inferred than that it might be 100 yards, or it might be 700 yards, according to the elevation of the piece. At no elevation, however, was there less than 100 yards' variation in its possible range, and at some elevations this difference exceeded 300 yards. So much for this primary point. Then came the point of accuracy, on which the revelations were still more astounding. At a distance of 150 yards, a target, about twice as high and twice as broad as a man, could, with very careful shooting, be hit three times out of four ; beyond that distance, notwithstanding that the musket was fired from a stand and every precaution employed to ensure steadiness and success, the result was *nil*. Nothing could be learnt at all, except that the target could never be hit and the balls could never be found. The mark was made twice as wide as before, but of ten shots at 250 yards not one struck."

With regard to the adoption of the Rifle, a book was published in 1800 by Ezekiel Baker, a gunsmith of Whitechapel, " Remarks on Rifle Guns," fully explaining the improved results, as to range and accuracy, obtainable in the flint lock muzzle-loader of his day. This appears to be the first popular illustrated work on the Rifle in English, although Benjamin Robbins, a Fellow of the Royal Society, had written and experimented on the subject about a quarter-of-a-century earlier, and a patent had actually been granted to A. Rotsipen for rifling as early as 1635. Although not much understood in this country, Rifles had been used for a long time on the continent. The Body Guard of Louis XIII. was armed with them, and in Germany they were made in the sixteenth century, with wheel-locks, and many fine specimens can be seen in the Wallace Collection and elsewhere.

Rifles were first used in the British service during the American War of Independence, 1775. The American troops, many of them armed with their small-bore hunting rifles, were found to have a great advantage over our troops armed with muskets ; so a number or German Jägers were enlisted armed with Rifles, which presumably they brought with them from Germany, and were sent to assist our troops. Colonel Hanger, who published a quaint book in 1814—"To all Sportsmen"—was a Captain in one of these Jäger Corps, and bears testimony to the accuracy of the American Rifles then in use. Other Rifles were used occasionally on our side, as Lieut.-Colonel Ferguson who was organizing loyalists in the South, and who was killed at the Battle of King's Mountain, 1780, was a noted rifleman and had invented a Breech-loading Rifle in 1776—of course, flint lock. This had a plug a little larger than the bore, screwed into the barrel just behind the touch-hole and under the breech end, and coming right through to the top where it was flush with the barrel ; the lower end was attached to a lever forming the trigger guard, by which it might be turned. The plug itself has a multi-threaded screw to give quick travel and on turning the trigger guard three-quarters round, the screw-plug descended below the bore of the barrel, so that powder and ball might be introduced into the chamber, and the screw-plug then returned to close the breech again.

"On the 1st of June, 1776, he made some experiments at Woolwich, before Lord Viscount Townshend, Lord Amherst,

FERGUSON FLINT LOCK BREECHLOADING RIFLE, MADE BY WILSON, MINORIES, LONDON.

General Harvey, Déragliers, and several other officers with the rifle gun on a new construction, which astonished all beholders. The like had never been done with any other small arms. Notwithstanding a heavy rain and the high wind, he fired during the space of four or five minutes at the rate of four shots a minute, at a target two hundred yards distance. He next fired six shots in one minute, and also fired (while advancing at the rate of four miles an hour) four times in a minute. He then poured a bottle of water into the pan and barrel of the piece when loaded so as to wet every grain of powder, and in less than half-a-minute he fired with it as well as ever, without extracting the ball. Lastly, he hit the bull's-eye lying on his back on the ground, incredible as it may seem to many, considering the variations of the wind and the wetness of the weather. He only missed the target three times during the whole course of the experiments."

This Rifle was probably an improvement on an older one which I have seen with the name of Warsop on it, in which the guard was attached to a single-threaded screw, which entered the barrel from below but did not come through to the top. Of course the screw had to be turned several times and then came away altogether.

We give an illustration of a somewhat similar rifle of a little later date, which was made by Durs Egg for George IV., when

BREECHLOADING FLINT LOCK RIFLE, BY DURS EGG.

Prince of Wales. In our illustration the barrel is shewn unscrewed rather more than is necessary for loading, in order to shew the ten-threaded breech screw, which is normally covered by the silver dust guard.

The following description of the defeat of Ferguson is from "The History of the British Army," by Hon. J. W. Fortescue, Vol. 3, pp. 322,3 (Macmillan), 1902 :—

"Accordingly, on the 7th September (1780) he (Cornwallis) advanced from Camden in two columns, the main body under his own command moving up the eastern bank, and the light troops and cavalry up the western bank of the Wateree. A third detachment under Major Ferguson at the same time moved up wide to the westward from Ninety-Six, with the object of raising recruits for the Militia, in which Ferguson still reposed a confidence which no one else could share. The progress of the main body was slow owing to scarcity of forage, and it was not until the 22nd that Cornwallis arrived and halted at Charlottetown. This district was a hotbed of revolution, and the British, while they remained in it, were harassed by incessant waylaying or shooting of the British despatch riders. Then, as usual, guerilla operations began again in rear of Cornwallis, and a fierce attack was made upon the post of Augusta, in Georgia, but was successfully repulsed with heavy loss to the Americans. The officer in command at Ninety-Six at once conceived the hope of cutting off this American party on its retreat to northward ; but finding that the chase led him too far afield, suggested the same idea to Ferguson. Eagerly embracing the project, Ferguson hurried to westward, until he had placed at least seventy miles between his detachment and Charlottetown, when he suddenly found himself threatened by a new and wholly unexpected enemy in the shape of three thousand settlers from the extreme backwoods, rough, half-civilized men whom no labour could tire, and whose rifles seldom missed their mark. Realizing his danger, Ferguson instantly sent messages for help to Charlottetown, and retreated towards that place with all haste. But every one of his messengers was shot down ; and the backwoodsmen, sending forward fifteen hundred picked men to ride after him, made so swift a pursuit as to leave him no hope of escape.

"On the 6th of October, therefore, he chose a strong position on a hill, known as King's Mountain, and turned to bay. This hill was covered with tall forest, beneath which the ground was strewn with huge boulders, while on one side it was rendered absolutely inaccessible by a precipice; and Ferguson seems never to have dreamed that he could not hold it for ever. On the following afternoon the advanced party of the backwoodsmen arrived about a thousand strong, and having tied up their horses, and divided themselves into three bodies, began to ascend the hill from three sides. Creeping up in silence, every man confident of his skill as a stalker and a marksman, the central division made its way up to the crest, where Ferguson met them with a volley and a charge with the bayonet. The backwoodsmen then fell back slowly, keeping their pursuers in check by a biting fire from behind the trees and boulders, until a storm of bullets in Ferguson's flank showed that a second division of his enemies was lying in wait for him. Turning at once upon them, Ferguson found that the third division of backwoodsmen, which had been hidden on the opposite flank, was firing steadily into his rear. Thus entrapped, the Militia found the odds too many against them. Still they fought hard until Ferguson was killed; and nearly four hundred of them had fallen killed and wounded before the remainder, rather more than seven hundred, laid down their arms. The whole loss of the backwoodsmen was eighty-eight killed and wounded, and the only marvel is that it should have been so great, for their exploit was as fine an example as can be found of the power of woodcraft, markmanship, and sportsmanship in war. The victors celebrated their success by hanging a dozen of their prisoners before they dispersed, in revenge for the execution at Augusta of certain militiamen who had been taken in arms against the British after accepting service with them. The victims were of course Americans, for it was not Mother Country and Colonies, but two Colonial factions that fought so savagely in Carolina."

6 AND 7. FORSYTH, SELF-PRIMING POCKET PISTOLS (ABOUT 1812).
8. "DEVOLVING PAN LOCK," FOR FLINT OR PERCUSSION, LACY & WITTON (ABOUT 1825).
9. PERCUSSION TUBE LOCK, MANTON'S PATENT (1818).
10. FORSYTH MAGAZINE PRIMER (1807).

The Rifle Brigade, 95th Regt., was raised in 1800, and was armed with Ezekiel Baker's Flint Lock Rifle, having seven grooves, with a quarter-turn in the 30-in. barrel of .615-in. calibre. A second battalion was raised in 1805, and the regiment formed a part of the celebrated Light Division in the Peninsular War. At the Battle of Waterloo, the Rifle Brigade did good service, wiping out some detachments of artillery. A German Rifle Regiment also occupied La Haye Sainte, but, running short of ammunition, through their regimental cart being stuck in a ditch, were turned out and cut up almost to a man.

Rifles, although much more accurate than the musket, took longer to load, owing to the force required to push the ball into the grooves and down the barrel, compared to the easy fit of the ball in the smooth-bore musket. In consequence of this slowness of fire, rifles were generally employed only by troops used as skirmishers, and probably the earliest occasions on which troops armed with rifles beat off serious charges of cavalry were the following, the account of which is taken from " Deane's Manual of Fire-Arms," 1858 :—

"When in 1812 the rear-guard of the Anglo-Portuguese army was pursued and attacked upon the retreat from Burgos to Valladolid by a numerous French cavalry, on which occasion two English cavalry brigades were brought into some confusion, the two light brigades of the King's German Legion became also engaged with the French Dragoons. These battalions had been 1000 strong, and one-third of these armed with the rifle. But the judicious principle had been pursued by their commanding officers throughout the operations, to keep the rifled arms as much as possible by the battalions, for which purpose all sick, wounded, and other absentees from the ranks,

left their rifles in exchange for a smooth bore musket.   Upon the
retreat in question, the battalions were so much reduced in strength
that the mounted officers could not be taken into the squares. Almost
all the men were thus armed with the rifle ; yet did they, nevertheless,
repel the frequently reiterated charges of the French cavalry ; and his
Majesty, the late King of Hanover, upon constituting from the *débris*
of those battalions the present Hanoverian Jäger Regiment of the
Guard, conferred upon them, as a memorial of their brilliant feat of
arms in the Peninsula, the permission to wear the name of the place
(Venta del Pozo) under the royal arms.   Major Jacobi, of the
Hanoverian service, in his critical remarks upon this arm, in 1829,
proved also amply, that even in its then condition, it yielded in
nothing, in the hands of those who knew how to use it, to the line
musket, with all its boasted celerity of fire.

"That this may not be deemed the citation of a mere isolated
case, we will refer here, also, to the action at Montmirail, where two
companies of Prussian riflemen, posted near Jeanvilliers, were
suddenly threatened by a numerous body of cavalry, which had
already broken some Prussian battalions of the line.   Captain New-
mann, the commanding officer of the Prussian Jägers, numbering 230
men only, in order to give his countrymen breathing time to re-
establish their order, advanced with sword-bayonets fixed, and a loud
hurrah against the enemy's cavalry.   The latter immediately detached
a squadron against them, which charged down upon the riflemen.
But so well directed, and so well sustained, was the fire of the latter,
who first opened, upon the word of their commandant, at fifty yards,
that the cavalry were obliged to clear the front, right and left.
Some few, it is true, closed upon the riflemen, and struck the

sword-bayonets from their rifles, and one Jäger had his czako cut from his head. But not a dragoon could get into the little Jäger column, and the cavalry retired. Could the smooth-bore and its vaunted bayonet have effected more?"

JOHN BLANCH

CHAPTER II.

BEFORE following the development of the Rifle, we must describe the most important invention ever made in connection with Fire Arms, which had already been patented, although as yet undeveloped.   The Rev. Alexander Forsyth, a Scottish clergyman, obtained a patent in 1807 for applying fulminate of mercury and other compositions, of which he mentions several, to the ignition of gunpowder by detonation by a blow, such as may be given by a gun lock suitably arranged.   Although the patent was opposed by several people claiming previous knowledge of this method of firing gunpowder, a law court held that as this was the first application for such a patent, it should be granted.   In the London Directory for 1812, we find, Forsyth & Co., Patent Gunmakers, at 10, Piccadilly ; and in 1818, at 8, Leicester Street, where they remained until 1852.

Forsyth, in his specification, says :—" First, as to the chemical plan and principles thereof, instead of permitting the touch-hole or vent of the pieces of artillery, fire-arms, mines, chambers, cavities, or places to communicate with the open air, and instead of giving fire to the charge by a lighted match, or by flint and steel, or by any other matter in a state of actual combustion applied to a priming in an open pan, I do close the touch-hole or vent by means of a plug or sliding piece, or other fit piece of metal or suitable material or materials, so as to exclude the open air, and to prevent any sensible escape of the blast or explosive gas or vapour outwards, or from the priming or charge, and as much as possible to force the said priming to go in the direction of the charge, and to set fire to the same, and not to be wasted in the open air ; and as a priming I do make use of some or one of those chemical compounds which are so easily inflammable as to be capable of taking fire and exploding without any actual fire being applied thereto, and merely by a blow, or by any sudden or strong pressure or friction given or applied thereto without extraordinary violence ; that is to say, for example, the salt formed of dephlogisticated marine acid and potash (or potasse), which salt is otherwise called oxymuriate of potash ; or I do make use of such of the fulminating metallic compounds as may be used with safety : for example, fulminating mercury, or of common gunpowder mixed in due quantity with any of the before-mentioned substances, or with an oxymuriatic salt as aforesaid, or of suitable mixtures of any of the before-mentioned compounds ; and these compounds, or mixtures of compounds, I find to be much better for priming than gunpowder used alone, which cannot be made to explode without some sparks or actual fire applied thereto, or else without such a degree of extraordinary and violent percussion as cannot conveniently be made use of in gunnery, or with any of the fire-arms or artillery that are in most general use.   But it is to be observed that I do not lay claim to the invention of any of the said compounds or matters to be used for priming, my invention in regard thereto being confined to the use and application thereof to the purposes of artillery and fire-arms as aforesaid ; and the manner of priming and exploding which I use is to introduce into the touch-hole or vent, or into a small and strong chamber or place between the said touch-hole and vent, and the plug or sliding piece, or other piece by which the communication with the external air is cut off, a small portion of some or one of the chemical compounds herein-before mentioned (for example, as for priming to a musket, about the eighth part of a grain), and when the required discharge is to be made I do cause the said chemical compound or priming to take fire and explode by giving a stroke or sudden and strong pressure to the same, communicated by and through the said plug or sliding piece, or other piece before mentioned or described, in consequence of which the fire of the priming is immediately communicated to the contents or charge placed within the said piece of artillery, fire-arm, mine, chamber, cavity, or place, and the discharge accordingly follows."

Although this appears to be the first practical application of detonating to fire-arms, fulminating substances had been known to chemists for a long time, and Pepys mentions them under date :— " November 11th, 1663. At noon to the Coffee-House, where, with Dr. Allen, some good discourse about physick and chymistry. And among other things I telling him what Dribble, the German doctor, do offer of an instrument to sink ships ; he tells me that which is more strange, that something made of gold, which they call in chymistry Aurum Fulminans, a grain, I think he said, of it put into a silver spoon and fired, will give a blow like a musquett, and strike a hole through the silver spoon downwards, without the least force upward ; and this he can make a cheaper experiment of, he says, with iron prepared."

The Forsyth Gun (group 1, fig. 2), which is most generally known, was both original and ingenious. In place of the priming pan outside the flash hole, a round plug having a small cavity

on the top which led to the flash hole, was fitted into the
barrel, and upon this plug was pivotted a magazine in the shape
of a small scent bottle with two necks opposite each other. In one
neck was mounted the striker rod held up by a light spring, and in
the other neck was a hole drilled down to the central plug, to contain
enough detonating powder for about twenty discharges, covered by a
sliding lid. In this lid, opposite the hole containing the powder, was
a similar hole filled up with a plug of horn or leather, to act as a
safety vent in case the entire contents were discharged by friction or
jar. This, perhaps, rarely happened ; but the great objection to the
system was the necessity of handling the loose detonating powder,
and although pellets or pilules of various compositions were tried,
as soon as the copper tube and copper cap had been invented, which
obviated the necessity of actually handling the detonating powder,
and cut it up into very small quantities, which were quite safe for
ordinary handling, and yet sufficiently sensitive when placed in position
on the lock and fired by a blow from the hammer, all attempts to
work with the loose powder were abandoned.

The operation of priming with the Forsyth Gun was, to rotate
the magazine primer until the hole containing the detonating powder
was over the small cavity in the top of the plug leading to the touch
hole, when a small quantity fell by gravity, assisted by the jar of the
primer being arrested in its rotation against a stop on the lock plate,
into the cavity in the plug. The primer was then rotated into its
opposite position, which brought the small striker rod over the cavity
now containing the detonating priming, and ready to be fired by the
fall of the cock on the striker. Another form of Forsyth Primer is
shewn in the Pistols in group 2.

The use of the term "hammer" is a little confusing, when writing or reading about old Guns, as in the flint lock, the part standing up and joined to the pan cover was called the "hammer," and the falling part, which carried the flint, was called the "cock.' When the flint lock disappeared, the name "hammer" was transferred to the falling piece or "cock." The "hammer" in the flint lock was sometimes called the "hen"; then we have the "cock" and the "hen." The trigger used to be called the "tricker," and survives from cross-bow days; it was the thing that did the trick.

In 1816, Joe Manton patented a Gun having a copper tube containing detonating powder, held "fore and aft" in a hole in the head of the hammer, which, in falling, struck the open end into a cavity in a plug, containing the flash hole, projecting from the barrel. In 1818, he improved on this, in another patent, by placing the copper tube in the flash hole itself, where it was held by a spring cover, and was struck in the middle through a hole in the cover by the hammer, which had an axe-shaped striking piece. This gave a very powerful flash and certain discharge, and could not blow the hammer back again as might happen with the other system; the only drawback being, that the fired tube might blow out to the right or left, with considerable force, to the danger of anyone near. In our illustration (group 2, fig. 9), even this is guarded against by a lip on the hammer. This system was admirably adapted for Punt Guns, where, owing to the thick wall of the barrel and the large size of powder desirable, which could not get into the flash hole, a powerful flash was essential.

The actual inventor of the copper cap has not yet been identified. Colonel Hawker seems to claim it for himself and Joe Manton

GROUP III.

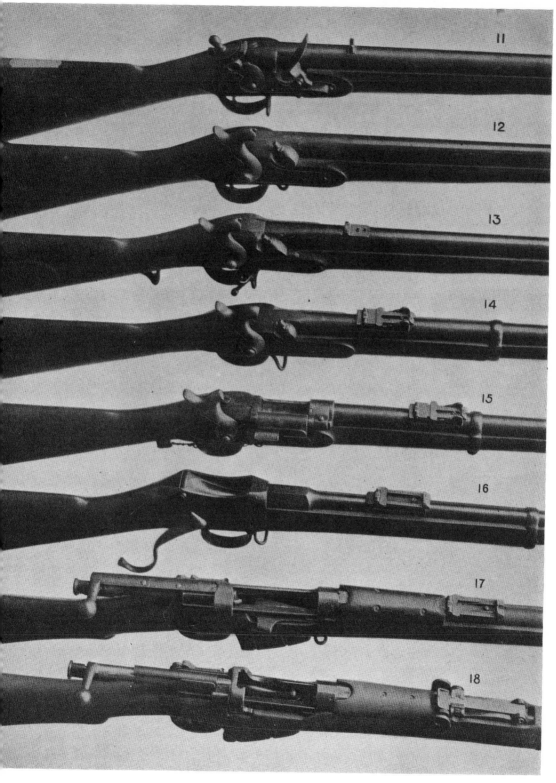

BRITISH ARMY WEAPONS, 1809-1909.

11. "BROWN BESS," FLINT LOCK MUSKET (1700-1842).	15. SNIDER RIFLE (1867).
12. PERCUSSION MUSKET (1839).	16. MARTINI-HENRY RIFLE, (1869).
13. BRUNSWICK (TWO GROOVED) RIFLE (1836).	17. LEE-METFORD RIFLE (1888).
14. ENFIELD RIFLE (1852).	18. SHORT LEE-ENFIELD RIFLE (1903).

together; others have claimed it for Joseph Egg, who appears to have introduced it; Wilkinson says it was first used by Mr. Joshua Shaw (an artist of Philadelphia) in 1814, and it was never patented. Although slight variations have been tried and patented over and over again, it still survives in its original thimble-shaped form as it appeared about 1821. Until about 1850, in this country it was generally placed upon a nipple outside the barrel, and then, after many attempts, means were found for fixing it to a cartridge and placing it inside the barrel, where it still forms the means of ignition in all small arms of the present day. Soon after the introduction of the copper cap, many inventions were patented for the purpose of placing the caps upon the nipple from a magazine attached either to the lock, stock, or barrel. They were generally operated by the movement of the hammer, but the advantages did not seem to justify the additional complication, and they seem to have been very soon abandoned. Other methods of continuous priming were also tried :— percussion pellets were fed from a magazine in Berenger's Patent, 1824 ; in 1825, Joe Manton patented a revolving pellet carrier ; in the same year there was a similar self-acting pellet magazine in the name of Downing ; in 1834, Baron Heurteloup patented a continuous primer consisting of a long tube of soft metal containing detonating powder, which was contained in a groove or chamber in the stock and fed forward by suitable mechanism, a portion of the tube being cut off by a cutting edge attached to the hammer, and the part so cut off was struck by the hammer itself immediately afterwards ; in 1836, Joseph Egg patented a self-acting magazine for supplying primers or detonating tubes to the touch hole.

In France, Messrs. Lepage, Debonbert, and Blanchard, of Paris, were prominently connected with the introduction of the percussion system of fire-arms.

In 1841, Baron Heurteloup improved his continuous primer by altering the mixture so that it would not continue to burn beyond the part cut off, and also rolled it up into a coil. In the same year Westley Richards describes a pasteboard primer covered with water-proof material, placed in a dove-tailed slot in a broad nipple (group 12, fig. 84). In 1843, Needham describes primers which may be contained in a groove in the stock, and pushed forward as required. In 1845, Charles James Smith had a somewhat similar design ; and, in the following year, Joseph Washington Tyson describes continuous primers in which the mixture is placed in little hollows, at regular intervals in a strip of paper ; this is covered with another thin strip of paper, and varnished. The strips of primers are coiled in a suitable case attached to the lock, and fed by a toothed wheel actuated by the lock motion. This was the principle of Maynard's Primer, 1843, applied to the Sharp Carbine, 1848 (group 4, fig. 19), and the Greene Carbine, 1854 (group 9, fig. 65). Sharpe's Carbine was afterwards fitted with a primer which fed shallow copper caps.

Group 2, fig. 8, shows a combination Flint and Percussion Lock, which could be used on either system, which was invented by Lacy and Witton who called it the Devolving Pan Lock.

In 1836, a Board appointed at Woolwich selected the two-grooved Brunswick Rifle, having a complete turn in the 30-in. barrel of .704-in. calibre (group 3, fig. 13). It fired a belted round ball, and was the first percussion rifle in the service. A few Lancaster rifles, also two-grooved, but firing a conical ball having two ribs on the sides, to fit the grooves, instead of the belt, this being the first conical ball rifle in the service, were issued to the first battalion of the Rifle Brigade in South Africa during the Kaffir War, 1846-52. With this exception, the Brunswick Rifle remained in the hands of the Rifle Brigade until they embarked for the Crimea, when they received the Minié Rifle of 1850, .702-in. calibre, with four grooves having one turn in 6 ft., then being issued to some of the line regiments as well as to the Rifle Brigade. Some of the regiments still had smooth bore percussion muskets, and some had rifled percussion muskets, which had been rifled as a temporary expedient in 1853. The percussion musket was of the same bore as Brown Bess (group 3, fig. 12), and was adopted in 1839. In 1840, the French Government made a grant for converting 700,000 flint lock muskets to percussion, and Germany had already adopted the system.

One of the Duke of Wellington's biographers (Mr. Gleig) says:—
"Touching Horse Guards' matters : it is quite a mistake to suppose that the Duke was an adherent of precedent merely for precedent's sake, that he opposed improvements, stuck up for Brown Bess, resisted Minié, etc. On the contrary, it was by his express direction that Anglesey, Master of the Ordnance, introduced 28,000 of the new weapon, but the F.M. wouldn't allow them to be called ' Rifles,' and struck his pen through the word, whenever he came across it, in a memorandum drawn up for him by Gleig. On the latter asking the meaning of the erasure, the unsophisticated old file rasped out that if the soldiers fancied themselves riflemen, they would become conceited and be wanting to be dressed in green or some other ' jack-a-dandy ' uniform."

The Minié Rifle, designed by a Captain in the French Army, fired a conical ball with an iron cup in the base, which caused it to expand

and fit the grooves on firing. As the ball went easily down the barrel, in its unexpanded condition, this greatly increased the rapidity of loading, as well as the accuracy.

The Minié Rifle was the result of some important experiments and improvements carried out in France, at first at the personal expense of Captain Delvigne, of the Guards, who in 1826 brought before the French Government an improved form of rifle which could be loaded as easily as a musket. The improvement consisted in giving the powder chamber a reduced diameter, so as to form a shoulder on which the ball rested, and on striking the ball two or three times with the ramrod, it was expanded into the grooves. These early experiments were with a round ball, which was at that time alone considered suitable for military purposes. The Delvigne system of chamber was adopted in the French rifle of 1838-42. In 1841 Delvigne took out an additional patent, in which he described a cylindro-conoidal ball with a hollow base. In 1844, Colonel Thouvenin, still adhering to the round ball, proposed an improvement, consisting in screwing a short pillar into the breech plug on which the ball could rest, and on being struck by the ramrod, expanded as in the Delvigne system. This suggestion was still awaiting adoption when Captains Minié and Tamasier, of the School of Musketry of Vincennes, suggested the adoption of a cylindro-conoidal bullet with a solid base. This was adopted by the French Government in combination with the pillar breech in 1846. Captain Tamasier also devised the decreasing depth of groove from the breech to the muzzle, which was found to give increased accuracy. He also discovered the advantage obtained by cutting two or three sharp-edged channels on the cylindrical rear end of the bullet, which by the resistance they offered in flight, tended to keep the point in coincidence with the trajectory, and thus greatly increase the accuracy at long range.

Minié's most important contribution to the problem referred to the bullet ; his first pattern had a solid coned base united by a short grooved neck to an ogival head, but after Tamasier had shewn the advantage of adding more grooves with a section like saw teeth presented to the front, he combined two of these with a hollow base in which an iron cap was inserted and driven half way up the bullet on firing, with a sphero-conoidal head.

In the English edition of the Minié Rifle, the exterior grooves, which were a characteristic feature of the Delvigne-Tamasier-Minié bullet, were omitted.

The Enfield Rifle (group 3, fig. 14) was barely ready when the troops left for the Crimea, but the manufacture was pushed on so energetically that a sufficient supply was available in a few months, large numbers being made by the trade here, and 25,000 in America. This rifle was the production of a committee appointed in 1852, and was manufactured at the Royal Small Arms Factory at Enfield, which was greatly enlarged and re-modelled, to meet the demands of the War with Russia, 1854-6, and equipped with American machinery. The rifles were not produced completely on the interchangeable system until 1858. The bore of the barrel was .577 inch with three grooves having one turn in 6 ft. 6 in., and the conical bullet without grooves had a hollow base, in which was placed a conical plug, at first made of boxwood, but afterwards of baked clay, to cause the expansion. This was a very excellent weapon for a muzzleloader, was manufactured in large quantities, and supplied to all troops

D

throughout the services. Its being served out to some of the native Indian Regiments, is reputed to have been the ostensible cause of the Indian Mutiny, 1857. The paper cartridges containing the powder and ball, were reported to be lubricated with pigs' fat and cows' fat. One end was generally broken off by the soldier's teeth, so as to pour the powder down the barrel loose. Although it appears that these Indian troops were told by their officers that they could break the cartridges with their hands, they protested that it was an attempt to injure their "caste," and mutinied. Owing to various political occurrences, a spirit of disaffection had been disseminated for some time previously, and the mutiny of one or two regiments led to a widespread insurrection, which took two years to suppress, and resulted in the government being taken over from the East India Company by the British Crown.

We will now leave the Service Rifle for a time, and go back to 1851, when the first Great International Exhibition was held in Hyde Park, London, in the building afterwards removed to Sydenham, and known as the Crystal Palace. This forms the half-way point in our review of the century, not only in time, but as a connecting link between the old system of Muzzleloading, and the modern system of Breechloading Fire Arms.

EZEKIEL BAKER

GROUP IV.

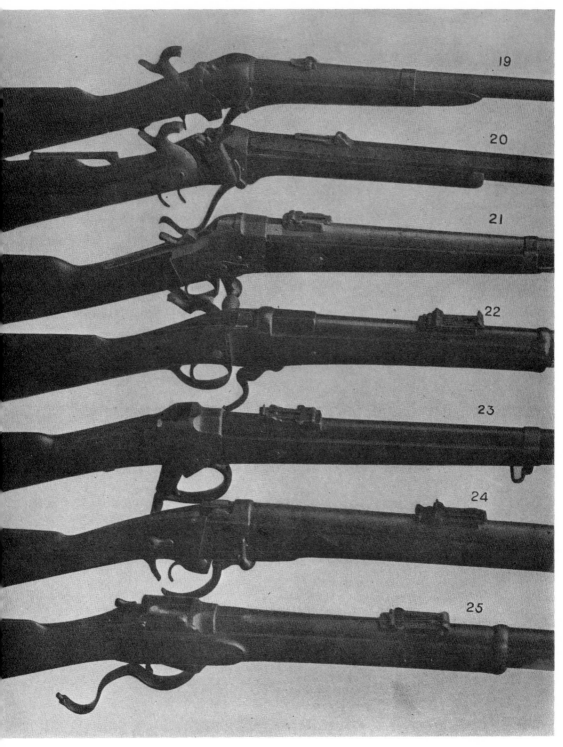

19. SHARP (U.S.A.) (1848), CAPPING BREECHLOADER, MAYNARD'S PAPER
    PRIMER.
20. SHARP (U.S.A.) (1852), CAPPING BREECHLOADER, FOR ORDINARY CAP,
    WAS ALSO MADE SELF-PRIMING WITH SHALLOW CAPS.
21. NAGANT BREECHLOADER.

22. HENRY BREECHLOADER (1865)
23. COMBLAIN BREECHLOADER (1869).
24. FARQUHARSON BREECHLOADER (1872).
25. BAILEY BREECHLOADER (1871).

CHAPTER III.

The Breechloading System. Revolvers. Capping Breechloaders. The Gastight Cartridge. Single Breechloading Military Rifles.

THE first English Patent for a breechloader was granted, in 1664, to Abraham Hall, whose gun is described as having "a hole at the upper end of the breech to receive the charge, which hole is opened and stopped by a piece of iron or steel that lies along the side of the piece, and movable by a ready and easy motion." In 1811 another Hall patented a breechloader in the U.S.A. (group 8, fig. 50), and 10,000 were made and used against the Indians from 1816 to 1827. Colonel Ferguson's Breechloading Rifle of 1776, has already been mentioned.

Previous to 1857, in this country at least, nearly all attempts at breechloading had the cap placed outside the barrel on a nipple, and a paper or skin cartridge containing powder and ball, within the barrel. Meantime many attempts had been made on the continent to produce a cartridge which should have a cap or primer attached to or contained in the cartridge itself.

Pauly, a Genevan gunsmith at Paris in 1808-12, invented a percussion breechloading gun in which a detonating paper cap was affixed to the cartridge, which was fired by a needle.

In 1831, Demondion patented a gun made by Robert, of Paris, in which the cartridge had a flattened percussion tube projecting, like a tail, from the back of it, which was struck by a hammer placed underneath the barrel.

In 1847, Houiller, another Paris gunsmith, patented the " Pin Fire " cartridge, in which a metal cap was placed in a wad at the base of the cartridge, and an anvil in the form of a long wire, rested in the cap and projected through both the cartridge and the barrel. This same inventor seems to have suggested also, both the rim fire and the central fire cartridges in a crude form. Upon the invention of the pin fire, which was the first "gas-tight" cartridge, it was immediately adopted by Lefaucheux, of Paris, the business successor of Pauly, who adapted his well-known gun to work with it. This gun is the direct progenitor of the modern double-barrelled Hammerless Ejector Gun. The Lefaucheux pin fire gun had been made in Paris for four or five years before the Exhibition, and with non-gastight cartridges some time before that. Immediately upon the invention of the gas-tight pin fire cartridge having a metallic base, it became an immense success and was in a few years in use all over the world. Although still opposed by several leading English makers, its advantages were so unmistakable that it carried all before it. *The Field*, October 16, 1858, wrote as follows :— " Messrs. Lang, Reilly, and Blanch have been overdone with orders and more than one gentleman we know has had great difficulty in meeting with what he wanted. It is therefore simply absurd to attempt to pooh-pooh the invention." The objections raised to it are stated in *The Dead Shot*, by Marksman, 1860, as follows :—

1. The breechloader does not shoot as strong, nor kill so far as the muzzle-loader, although allowed a quarter of a drachm of powder extra.

2. The breechloader is of necessity much heavier than a muzzleloader of the same gauge.

3. It is more expensive as regards ammunition, and also as to the gun itself, by reason of its not lasting so long, and its greater liability to get out of repair than a muzzleloader.

4. The recoil on discharge is heavier and the report louder than those produced by a muzzleloader.

5. The penetration of wet and damp, in rain, fogs, or mists, between the false breech and barrels, and often into the charge itself, cannot be avoided in the breechloader.

6. There is obviously a greater risk of bursting, indeed, the safety of the breech-loader, after much usage, becomes doubtful, by reason of the escape of gas between the false breech and barrels; particularly after the trying vibrations of heavy charges.

7. The time and trouble required in making the cartridges before going shooting is very considerable, and it is with one peculiar form of cartridge only that the breechloader can be used; and if purchased of the gunmaker, they are far more expensive than loose powder and shot.

8. The cartridges must be carried in a strong case with divisional compartments for each cartridge. In the event of their being carried loose they become damaged; and the danger of so carrying them is excessive, by reason of the results which may ensue in the event of a fall or accident in getting over a hedge, or otherwise, whereby a blow or friction is given to the metal pin which explodes the cap.

9. The extra weight incurred in being obliged to carry a sufficient number of cartridges for a day's sport in a very cumbersome leather case, with iron compartments, considerably exceeds the ordinary weight of powder flask and shot pouch, with ammunition for a similar amount of sport.

Another of the principal defects in the breechloader is the flat surface of the breech, which scientific and practical experimenters have proved to be erroneous, by reason of the much greater power and extra force which may be obtained from the conical interior form of breech, the rule being that " force cannot be expended and retained also," and, as it must of necessity be expended to a certain degree by explosion and recoil on a flat surfaced breech, therefore extra powder is required to produce like effects to those which result from the conical breech, the recoil is also considerably greater on a flat surface than on a tapering one. (This refers to the Patent Concave Breech Plug of Henry Egg, 1787.) "Joints, joinings, slides, and bolts, are all inferior to a well made screw, as regards soundness of the breech. A perfectly solid breech, free from all suspicious joinings, crevices, and openings, must be by far the safer and more effective in any instrument in which so searching a substance as gunpowder has to be compressed and exploded."

Although most of these objections have proved to be groundless, or of little practical consequence, the fact remains that, as shown at many public trials, the early breechloaders did not shoot as well as the best muzzleloaders. Curiously enough, the same thing had been shown by Colonel Hawker and others on the introduction of the detonator, it was not equal to the flint ; which shows to what refinement the boring and chambering had been adjusted, by long experience, to the means of ignition, and that a radical change in this respect required adjustments in other particulars to produce equal results to the older form. In the case of the breechloader, certain new conditions arose ; in the first place, the cartridge had to have the end turned in upon the wad to secure the charge when handling or travelling, and this required considerable work to be done by the powder in opening it, which, perhaps, accounts for the extra quarter drachm required. But the most important alteration was the cutting off of the three-quarters of an inch of barrel behind the powder charge, which in the muzzleloader was occupied by the screw plug. If we consider for a moment a paper tube well pasted together and the size of a gun barrel, and ask ourselves whether it would be easier to burst

LEFAUCHEUX BREECHLOADER AT 1851 EXHIBITION.

LEFAUCHEUX REVOLVER AT 1851 EXHIBITION.

it open, by an internal strain, close to its open end, or three-quarters of an inch farther up the tube, we shall realize at once that, for the open end of the tube to stand the same strain as it will farther up, the edge must be considerably strengthened. This explains why it is seldom desirable to convert a muzzleloader into a breechloader, for not only must the screw-threaded part be cut off, thus taking the support of the threaded part (which was not itself under the stress of the explosion) away from the part forming the powder chamber and thus weakening it, but this vital part itself must be again much weakened by cutting out an amount of metal corresponding to the thickness of the paper cartridge case, so that the wad on leaving the cartridge shall fit the bore of the gun. In the breechloader, the paper caulkage at the bottom of the cartridge case carried the base of the explosion chamber a quarter of an inch up the barrel, but this did not compensate for the three-quarters of an inch cut off. The consequence was, in the early breechloaders, the barrels being of very little more than the usual thickness of the muzzleloader, round the explosion chamber, there was undue expansion, with weak shooting, and a tendency to gape at the breech on firing, and, perhaps, split the rim of the cartridge. Considering that the lump under the barrels was only brazed into a V-shaped trough without any dovetailing, and that there was at first only one grip (and that far forward) it is a wonder that there were not more accidents. Under modern conditions of powder pressure, they would not have been safe for a single day. Of course, this condition of weakness was speedily remedied by trumpeting out the barrels and thus giving reinforcement to the breech, by dovetailing the lumps into the barrels as well as brazing them, and by fitting stronger and better placed holding-down bolts.

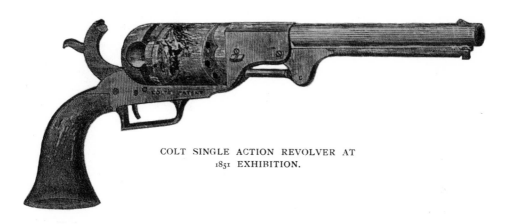

COLT SINGLE ACTION REVOLVER AT
1851 EXHIBITION.

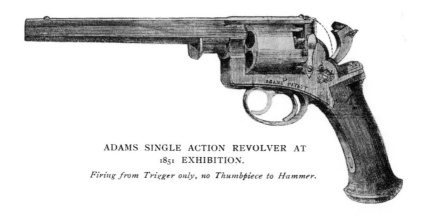

ADAMS SINGLE ACTION REVOLVER AT
1851 EXHIBITION.

Firing from Trigger only, no Thumbpiece to Hammer.

It is almost needless to say that the modern breechloader, especially since the introduction of choke boring and smokeless powder, shoots much better than a muzzleloader.

A glance at the Catalogue of the 1851 Exhibition will give a good idea of the general progress of Fire Arms to that date, and, as the official catalogue is now somewhat scarce, it seems of sufficient interest to reproduce those entries relating to Small Arms, as both the names of the exhibitors and the systems exhibited are illustrative for our purpose.

SMALL ARMS AT THE 1851 EXHIBITION, LONDON.

(From the Official Catalogue)

GREAT BRITAIN :—

59—W. Greener, Birmingham ; double guns and rifles, harpoon guns, rocket gun and lines for use in shipwrecks, patent stanchion gun for wild fowl shooting, military musket and rifle ; laminated steel, &c.

200—Wilkinson & Son, 27, Pall Mall ; gun, with spiral recoil spring, for wild fowl shooting, fowling pieces, rifle, &c.

203—Witton, Daw & Co., 57, Threadneedle Street ; rifles for India and Africa, fowling piece, duelling pistols.

205—Hawker, Col. P., Longparish House, near Whitchurch, Hants ; a stanchion gun, with improved waterproof ignition, forged and stocked on a new principle, models of two-handed punts containing gun, gear, &c., for wild fowl shooting.

206—Brazier, J. & R., Wolverhampton ; specimens of gun manufacture; double gun-tube locks ; double rifle locks, musket percussion locks, &c.

207—Potts, T. H., Haydon Square, Minories; double barrel guns, with improved breeches, bolted triggers, &c.

209—Moore & Grey, 78, Edgware Road ; double fowling pieces, two grooved rifles and pistols.

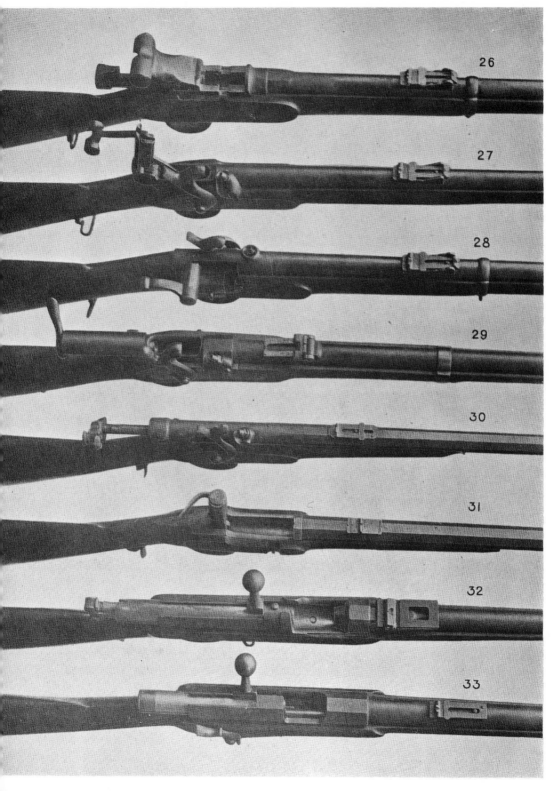

26

27

28

29

30

31

32

33

BENSON & POPPENBURG BREECHLOADER (1866).
COOPER (COOPER & GOODMAN) (1860) CAPPING BREECHLOADER.
GRAINGER (1860) CAPPING BREECHLOADER.
FRENCH CAPPING BREECHLOADER, SIMILAR TO LANCASTER (1854).

30. TERRY (CALLISHER & TERRY) (1853) CAPPING BREECHLOADER.
31. NEEDHAM NEEDLE-FIRE BREECHLOADER (1852).
32. NEEDLE RIFLE OF 1869.
33. NEEDLE RIFLE, WITH OUTSIDE COCKING PIECE.

214—Robinson, A., 41, Whitcomb Street, Haymarket; best Damascus gun barrels.

215—Gibbs, G., Clare Street, Bristol; improved reg. double-barrel gun, with protector against wet.

216—Beattie, J., 205, Regent Street; two-groove rifle, double gun, duelling pistols, &c.

217—Manton & Son, 6, Dover Street, Piccadilly; double guns, double rifle, duelling pistols, &c.

218—Needham, W. & J., 26, Piccadilly; patent self-priming gun, self-priming musket, to use the military flange cap; safety stop-lock gun, game registers, double and single guns to load at the breech, self-loading carbine.

219—Boss, T., 73, St. James' Street; a central fire double and other guns.

220—Beckwith, H., 58, Skinner Street, Snow Hill; fowling pieces, blunderbusses, and other fire arms.

221—Bentley & Son, 12, South Castle Street, Liverpool; double patent central fire percussion guns.

222—Trulock & Son, 9, Dawson Street, Dublin; double bar guns, centripetal double gun, pistols, &c.

223—Deane, Adams & Deane, 30, King William Street, E.C.; patent spiral raised rib rifles, patent safety stop lock guns, patent gun locks, fowling pieces, Indian and African rifles, pistols, &c.

224—Parker, Field & Sons, 233, Holborn; fowling and rifle guns, pistols, air-gun, musket, fusil, carbine, &c.

225—Eley, W. & C., 38, Broad Street, Golden Square; illustrations of the manufacture of patent wire cartridges and percussion caps, gun wadding.

226—Lang, J., 7, Haymarket; guns, rifles, pistols and revolvers, patent walking stick gun, with rifle and shot barrels, &c.

228—Golding, W., 27, Davies Street, Berkeley Square (Joe Manton's old shop); double sporting gun with improvements.

230—Woodward, J., 64, St. James' Street; fowling piece with detached waterproof lock.

231—Yeomans & Sons, 67, Chamber Street, Goodman's Fields ; an assortment of muskets.

232—Egg, H., 1, Piccadilly ; self-priming and barrel copper cap fowling pieces.

233—Fairman, 68, Jermyn Street ; double cross-eyed gun, double gun in soft state, single gun, single rifle, two grooved, &c.

234—Osborne, C., 1, Lichfield Street, Birmingham; improved central fire double guns with chain-twist barrels, bar slide, double and single guns, tube single gun, large single gun with Colonel Hawker's improved ignition, improved alarm gun, pistols, &c.

235—Goddard, S. A., Birmingham ; fowling guns, American ducking gun, pattern and common African musket, Californian protector gun, invented by the exhibitor.

236—Rigby, W. & J., 24, Suffolk Street, Dublin ; guns and rifles, double and single, rifle and revolving pistols, &c.

237—Reilly, E. M., New Oxford Street ; improved guns, rifles, pistols, air guns, &c.

238—Davidson, D., Captain, Bombay Army ; rifles and pistols with telescopic sights and bored for grooved bullets.

238A—Watkins & Hill, Charing Cross ; rifle with telescope.

239—Bull, J., Bedford ; double-barrel gun, with the modern improvements.

240—Richards, Westley & Son, Birmingham ; rifles, double tiger guns, punt gun, pistols, &c.

241—Cooper, J. R. & Co., 24, Legge Street, Birmingham ; patent self-cocking pocket pistol, revolving pistols, ladies' pistols, &c.

242—Walker, R., Graham Street, and Broad Street, Birmingham ; specimens of percussion caps, metallic gun wadding, &c.

243—Townsend, J., 11 & 12, Sand Street, Birmingham ; improved rifle and walking-stick air guns.

245—Hart, H., 54, New Canal Street, Birmingham ; guns and pistols ; specimens of gun barrel manufacture in every state, from the old horse-nail stubs of earliest period to the latest improvements.

246—Brooks & Son, 28, Russell Street, Birmingham ; fowling pieces, rifles, revolving gun, military guns, South American (Buenos Ayres) and Spanish carbines, African trading guns, Dane guns, pistols, &c.

247—Tipping & Lawden, Birmingham; illustration of gun barrel manufacture, rifles, guns, pistols, air guns, &c.

249—Powell & Son, Carr's Lane, Birmingham ; double-barrelled rifle and gun ; pistols, improved safety trigger guard, pair of lock actions, &c.

250—Winton, H., 53, Cleveland Street, Birmingham ; improved safety guns.

252—Hoskins, J., 31, Frith Street, Soho Square ; double gun with safety, on a new and simple principle.

253—Davis, J., 1, Duke Street, North Parade, Bath ; soldier's musket, substituting the blade of the bayonet for the ramrod.

255—Fletcher, T., 161, Westgate Street, Gloucester ; patent safety gun, with various improvements.

256—Forsyth & Co., Leicester Street, Leicester Square ; patent safety gun, &c., original percussion gun as invented by Forsyth, containing a reservoir of powder.

257—Erskine, J., Newton Stewart, Scotland ; two guns, newly invented to prevent accidental discharge, with complete waterproof for the cap.

258—Rippingille, E., 87, Albany Street, Regent's Park ; an improved gun lock with stock.

259—Haswell, R., 12, Upper Ashley Street ; air pistol on a new principle.

260—Needham, H., 4, Vine Street, Regent's Park ; self-priming fowling piece.

261—Brider, J., 4, Clifton Cottages, Denmark Street, Camberwell ; telescope loading rod for fire-arms.

262—Brider, G., 30, Bow Street, Covent Garden ; rifle mallet for hot climates.

263—Baker, T. K., 88, Fleet Street ; improved patent gun lock for preventing accidents from fire-arms.

264—Golden & Son, Huddersfield ; Bentley's patent double gun with improved locks, &c.

E

265—Webster, W., Hampstead Road ; fuzee musket.

267—Mortimer, T. E., 97, George Street, Edinburgh ; double rifle, fowling piece, Highland pistols, improved conical and other balls, &c.

269—Hodges, R. E., 44, Southampton Row ; patent application of india-rubber to projectile purposes.

270—Parsons, W., Swaffham, Norfolk ; improved double guns, &c.

277—Joyce, F. & Co., 57, Upper Thames Street ; improved anti-corrosive waterproof gun caps, percussion tube primers, chemically prepared gun waddings, patent wire cartridges, &c.

278—Grainger, J., Wolverhampton ; tube and bar-action gun and rifle gun locks.

280—Gardner, W. T., 22, Mead Row, Lambeth ; model of a ship's gun loaded at the breech.

281—King, T. J., 16, Whiskin Street, Des. ; pistols inlaid with gold and silver.

284—Walker, Sarah, & Co., 12, Legge Street, Birmingham ; percussion caps and patent metallic gun waddings.

287—Squires, W., Cottage Grove, Mile End ; new rifle calculated to project a ball to a great distance with a small charge.

288—McGettrick, F., 81½, Philip Street, Kingsland Road ; model of a war engine able to fire 10,900 charges of ball cartridges in ten minutes.

297—Cherrett, D., Grosvenor Mews, Berkeley Square ; an improved two-groove rifled pistol, with invisible lock. Throws a ball 250 yards, and can be used as a pistol, or from the shoulder.

AMERICA :—

236—Allen, G. F., Utica ; telescopic rifle.

307—Pecare & Smith, New York ; self-locking and repeating pistols, with stocks of ivory and rosewood, mounted with steel and gold.

321—Colt, S., Hertford ; specimens of fire-arms.

328—Robbins & Lawrence, Windsor ; Vermont rifles with their various parts made to interchange.

347—Palmer, W. R., New York ; specimens of two rifles.

AUSTRIA :—

112—Meyer & Co., Innspruck; a Tyrolese rifle, exhibited for its superior qualities and cheapness.

116—Kehlners Nephew, Prague; a pair of pistols for shooting at a target.

118—Schamal, F., Prague; an air pistol.

119—Micheloni, G., Milan; double-barrelled fowling piece.

BELGIUM :—

143—Ancion & Co., Liege; guns, muskets, pistols, rifles and other weapons.

144—Thonet, J., Liege; gun, ornamented with gilt silver; a pair of Scotch pistols, incrusted.

145—Lepage, Liege; complete collection of fire-arms, double-barrelled guns, rifles, holster pistols, duelling pistols, pocket pistols.

146—Plomdeur, N., Liege; guns and pistols.

147—Malherbe, L., Liege; double-barrelled and other guns, rifles, pistols, &c.

148—Ledent, M., Liege; a lock for all sorts of guns.

149—Doutrewe, F. J., Liege; a " needle " gun.

150—Bernemolin, N., & Brothers, Liege; double-barrelled gun and pistols.

151—Lardinois, N. C., Liege; rifle, with accessories, Swiss style, double-barrelled with accessories, made except the barrel and locks by Mr. C. Lenders.

152—Tinlot, M., Liege; a double-barrelled gun with stock carved style Louis XI.

153—Dehousse, Liege; guns and pistols.

154—Falisse & Rapmann, Liege; arms and percussion caps, fire-arms, rifles, guns, pistols.

155—Tourey, H., Liege; collection of fire-arms.

158—Montigny & Fusnot, Brussels; three infantry guns (Montigny system).

DENMARK :—

14—Jensen, N. S., Naval Arsenal, Copenhagen ; a rifle with an oval barrel, to discharge a conical ball, specimen of cartridge.

[The oval bore is mentioned by Col. Beaufoy, "Schloppetaria," 1808 ; it was also adopted by Capt. Berner, in Brunswick, 1855 ; and Lancaster oval bore percussion rifles were issued to our sappers and miners, about 1856.]

FRANCE :—

58—Bertonnet, Paris ; guns of several kinds, damasked and carved rifle gun, drawing room pistol ; pistol with carved barrel, &c.

166—Devisme, Paris ; muskets, various fire and side arms, patented.

215—Flobert, Paris ; guns, muskets and pistols, patented.

418—Berger, F., St. Etienne ; fancy fowling pieces of various kinds.

491—Dandoy-Maillard, Lucq & Co., Maubeuge ; military weapons.

509—Fontenau, F., Nantes ; Percussion gun, with under box and a safety hammer.

519—Gevelot & Lemaire, Paris ; percussion caps.

618—Mathieu, L., Paris ; fire-arms.

947—Peigne, V. J., Nort ; new self-priming gun.

1133—Caron, A., Paris ; a Parisian and other guns and pistols.

1158—Claudin, Paris ; guns and pistols of a new construction.

1251—Goddet, A., Paris ; pistol and fowling piece with two and four barrels.

1308—Lefaucheux, Paris ; different sorts of guns.

1364—Moutier le Page, Paris ; guns, carbines, pistols, swords, &c.

1451—Ronchard-Siauve, St. Etienne ; double-barrel gun, fifteen shades.

1546—Beringer, B., Paris ; five fowling pieces of various prices.

1547—Bernard, L., Passy ; Damascus gun and pistol barrels.

1611—Gastinne-Rennette, Paris ; guns, carbine, unfinished gun barrels, pistols (for practice) in their cases, and small fancy pistols ; model of a machine to load pistols and serving as a meter.

1628—Houiller, B., Paris; a box of pistols.

1681—Prelat, Paris; brace of pistols with carved and chased gold mountings, five-barrelled pistols (charges fired separately).

1712—Duclos, J., Paris; six guns and twelve pistols.

1724—Lagreze, Paris; five guns.

GERMANY :—

60—Gehrmann, T., Berlin; priming pin rifle gun, rifle, double-barrelled gun.

61—Ludlich, Posen; rifle.

62—Ohle, E. F., Breslau; shot tubes made by the hydraulic press (tinned inside and outside).

63—Grzybowski, H., Potsdam; rifle in rosewood.

64—Kehl, J. C., Berlin; pistols in box.

478—Schaller, C., Suhl; rifle, with cast-steel barrel, iron trimming; gold hunting piece (engraved) with iron spring lid—it is loaded at the stock and has a contrivance for pointed bullets (Spitz-kugeln).

479—Sauer & Son, Suhl—A double gun and single rifle, a single rifle ornamented with silver.

481—Pistor, G. & W., Schmalkalden; rifle gun with barrel of German cast steel.

638—Dreyse & Collenbusch, Sommerda; percussion caps.

677—Krupp, F., Essen; steel gun, 6-pounder complete, steel cuirass and one tried by being fired at with six different bullets.

678—Teutenberg, L., Huesten; rifle with seven barrels, which can all be fired and loaded at once, particularly applicable for shooting wild fowl, &c.

698—Anschutz, R., Zella; gun and rifle barrels of common wire and flower damask, of fine Paris and fine flower (Turkish) damask, of fine chain damask, of Laminette and Gotha damask, of fine steel wire and iron damask; the iron for the steel is made in Zella of sparry iron-stone, obtained from the district of Schmalkalden.

699—Brecht, A., Weimar; rifles with fine damask barrels and walnut-tree stock, ranged for pointed and round balls, &c.; the iron employed is from Thuringia, the barrels from Lutsorh.

701—Konig, C. G., & Sons, Coburg ; pair of octagon pistols inlaid with gold in the Gothic style, the stocks of elm (Ulmus campestris) inlaid with silver.

702—Sauerbrey, L., Zella Blasii ; double rifle of solid cast-steel. Both barrels are bored in a converging direction, to one aim, in such a manner as to direct the balls to the same mark ; it carries pointed and also round balls, &c.

801—Blancke, E., Naumberg ; double-barrelled gun, joint bullet rifle.

855—Schilling, Suhl ; pair of fine target pistols.

887—Gleichauf, B., Bockenheim ; a needle pistol with twelve barrels.

BAVARIA :—

20—Heinlein, C. V., Bamberg ; a rifle, highly finished, carved and ornamented in the old German style.

21—Kuchenreuter, T. J., Regensburg ; two pairs of rifle pistols in rosewood cases, highly finished and carry 240 yards.

WURTEMBURG :—

15—Royal Gun Manufactory, Oberndorf ; gun for infantry, rifle with bayonet, and common rifle ; made of cast-steel.

SAXONY :—

32—Thuerigen, F. T., Meissen ; a gun with double barrel on a new percussion principle.

FRANKFORT-ON-THE-MAINE :—

6—Weber & Schultheis ; single and double-barrelled rifles.

HESSE :—

18—Dichore, A., Giessen ; rifle, 4 ft. 10 in. long, inlaid with gold and silver.

HANOVER :—

3—Tanner, C. D. ; brace of pistols in case ; gun with two double barrels, in case ; rifle in case.

LUBECK :—

5—Fischer, Carl August ; guns, double-barrelled rifle with case, fowling piece, and rifle.

MECKLENBURG-SCHWERIN :—

2—Schmidt, J., Güstrow ; three guns.

On looking down the list of names it is rather a shock to find Joe Manton's old shop at 27, Davies Street, in the possession of a stranger, W. Golding. Alas! the most celebrated British gunsmith of the first half of the nineteenth century, who had received the highest price then known for his work, seventy guineas for a double gun, was unable to carry on, owing to heavy losses (so I have understood) in connection with the legal defence of some of his many patents. He had two actions with Forsyth, and I believe lost both, as Forsyth's was held to be a master patent. Joe Manton died in 1835, aged 69, one year after John Manton, who died in 1834. Colonel Hawker, in his sixth edition 1830, of his " Guide to Young Sportsmen," chapter 1, says :—" Joe Manton, the life and soul of the trade, obliged to sell off everything in Hanover Square, then rallied at Marylebone Park-house, where all was again soon wreck and confusion," and a few pages farther on :—" N.B. Since writing thus far, who should I meet but Joe Manton ? and what should he announce to me but that he had set up again (at Burwood Place in the Edgware Road) and was coming out with a new patent." Colonel Hawker's book, which went through about ten editions, is certainly the most delightful book ever written in English, on guns and gunnery, combining laborious investigation, lengthened personal experience, and charm, and has never been equalled by any of his successors. Since his time we have had *The Field* newspaper, established about 1853, as a sort of weekly Colonel Hawker to chronicle and criticise the later developments of small arms ; and a few useful books, but without his charm, the two best being "The Gun and its Development," by W. W. Greener, 8th edition (Cassell), 1907, and "The Book of the Rifle," by Hon. T. F. Fremantle (Longman's), 1901.

At the Exhibition, it is noticeable that although Messrs. F. Joyce and Co., and W. and C. Eley, and other wadding and cap makers were there, there is no mention of breechloading cartridges, the wire cartridges mentioned by Messrs. Eley being only shot enclosed in wire and paper for loading muzzleloading guns. Neither do Messrs. Reilly or Lang, two of the earliest firms to introduce breechloading sporting guns in this country, make mention of them. In 1855 a Lang Breechloader is described by "Stonehenge" in "British Rural Sports." Needham does mention double and single guns to load at the breech, but the Needham breechloader, introduced about 1850 (group 15, fig. 112) was a modification of the "Needle gun," and used a self-consuming cartridge with a wad at the back, covered with thin zinc, and holding a cap, the remains of which were pushed forward after firing, by the next cartridge inserted, the gun not being fitted with an extractor at first. Double guns with "needle fire" had been made for some time on the continent, but had the disadvantage of a considerable escape of gas through the needle hole into the lock work, which of course required cleaning whenever used ; these guns were hammerless and of good outline, one of which is shown in our illustration (group 1, fig. 4).

Although Bentley, Boss, and Osborne showed central fire double guns, these were not breechloaders, and the term either refers to guns similar to the one illustrated (group 1, fig. 4) or else some special form of breech plug, for conveying the flash of the cap to the centre of the powder charge, in which sense the term had already been used.

Forsyth and Co. showed the original percussion gun, as invented by Mr. Forsyth 1807, containing a reservoir of powder for ignition.

GROUP VII.

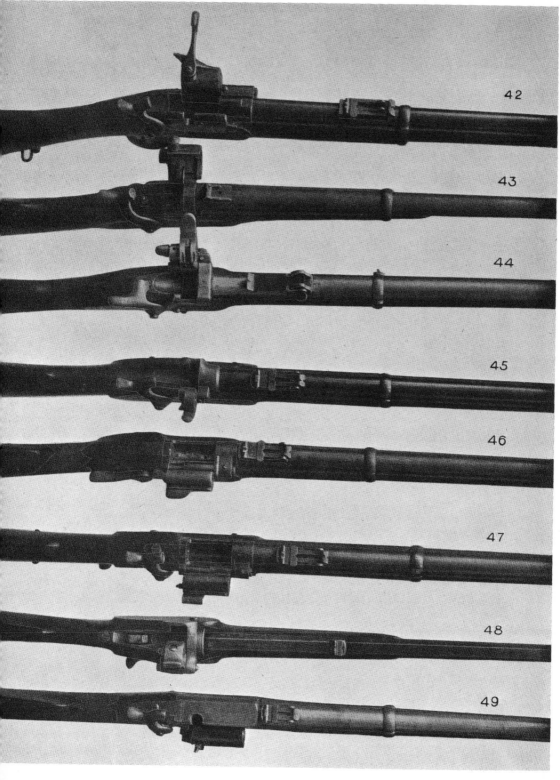

42

43

44

45

46

47

48

49

SHEDDEN BREECHLOADER (1867).
DAY BREECHLOADER (U.S.A.) (1864).
RUSSIAN CONVERTED BREECHLOADER (1866).
CORNISH BREECHLOADER (1866).

46. NEWARK'S SNIDER BREECHLOADER (1867).
47. SNIDER BREECHLOADER (1862).
48. SOPER BREECHLOADER (1868).
49. LEECH CAPPING BREECHLOADER (1861), LOADED IN THE BLOCK.

W. T. Gardner showed a model of a ship's gun loaded at the breech, but as he says nothing about a cartridge we may conclude it was fired by a cap or primer. Locks for cannon were made in the flint lock days and were occasionally fitted, at the Captain's personal expense I believe, to a few of the most efficient ships in the British Navy. The lock was generally mounted on the gun, but in some cases it was fixed like a pistol on the end of a walking stick and fired by a long trigger. Percussion caps and tubes were tried, and then the well-known " Friction Tube," which does not require a lock, and has remained in use until quite recently.

F. McGettrick astonishes us with a model of a war engine—he does not call it a gun—able to fire 10,900 charges of ball cartridges in ten minutes. As his name does not appear in the Patent lists under small arms, probably the invention was never patented or taken beyond the model stage. A few years later, however, in 1855, W. Treeby patented a very remarkable " chain gun," which it is a wonder was not developed into something to precede the Gatling and other machine guns operated by hand. This consisted in a rifle for the shoulder or preferably mounted on a carriage, constructed with a chain of chambers containing the charges and with a nipple attached to each, which were brought successively into line with the barrel and fired, being fed forward by suitable gear worked from the hammer, at the rate of 33 shots a minute. It was only necessary to unlock the barrel, pull up the hammer, replace the barrel, and pull the trigger until all the charges were fired, when a fresh loaded chain could be introduced. The inventor seems to have met with no encouragement from the Government, and although the *United Service Gazette* of June 4th, 1859, gave him an article in which it said :—"Thus, if an enemy were advancing up a sea beach, or across a field at a distance of 400 yards, one hundred of these chain rifles, in the hands of good marksmen, would annihilate 5,000 men in two or three minutes !" Nothing more seems to have been heard of it.

On the whole the British guns at the 1851 Exhibition are described in "The Crystal Palace and its Contents, an illustrated Cyclopædia of the Great Exhibition of 1851," from which our illustrations are taken, in the following terms :— "There were not exhibited many remarkable novelties, the chief merit consisting in excellence of workmanship and high finish."

Among the foreign weapons at the 1851 Exhibition were several very remarkable breechloaders, notably the Needle Rifle and the Lefaucheux Sporting Gun. We have an illustration of the latter, a single pin fire gun ; also a pin fire revolver by Lefaucheux, with its cartridge, and an English and an American muzzleloading revolver by way of comparison. The form of the French revolver is a very old design, known as a "Pepper Pot," and was unusual at that date, and the general type of Lefaucheux pin fire revolver, which is still after 50 years extensively made, has a barrel and cylinder of five or six chambers. Revolving barrels, or a fixed barrel and revolving cylinder, had been used even before the flint lock days, when the powder was fired by a smouldering rope match held in a piece of bent iron pivotted in the middle, called a "Serpentine," the lower part of which formed the trigger. Flint lock revolving pistols were made to a small extent, and the Collier, 1818, represents the highest point reached. The Collier Revolver (group 17, fig. 119) was provided with a cone joint connecting the chamber of the cylinder with the barrel, which required a backward and forward motion to be given to the cylinder, as well as a revolving one, and also a moveable support to the cylinder during firing. In the Collier, the cylinder of which was drawn back, turned, and again pushed forward by hand, the support was supplied by a small steel wedge, which was pushed into its place behind the cylinder by the fall of the tumbler. A breechloading revolver on a similar principle was invented by Nagant, patented in 1894, and was adopted by Russia.

Even flint lock repeating pistols were attempted, one which was made for Lord Nelson by H. W. Mortimer (group 17, fig. 120) could be fired about seven times, being reloaded by means of a lever, lying along the left side of the stock, and attached to a pivotted breech piece, the powder chamber in which was normally in register with the barrel, but on being rotated by the lever, was successively brought opposite to a receptacle for balls, and a powder magazine. The powder chamber had a partition in the middle which prevented a ball from entering, but after it had passed the ball receptacle, another cavity in the revolving breech piece came opposite the ball, into which it could enter, the cavity being conical and larger than the ball. When the breech piece was revolved in the reverse direction, the barrel being pointed downwards, the ball fell from this cavity into the chamber of the barrel, and when the breech piece had completed its return movement, the powder chamber in it was brought in line with the ball. A grooved roller extended from the axis of the breech piece and entered the pan of which it formed the bottom, and when rotated, connected with another small powder magazine, and received a small charge each time it was operated.

The lever also closed the pan cover and cocked the lock, one forward and backward movement of it being all that was required to "make ready" for another shot.

The invention of the percussion cap greatly simplified the problem for revolvers, and Colonel Colt in America, with his single action, and Adams and others in England, with double action of trigger, quickly perfected it into a practicable weapon. The old percussion "Pepper Pots" of 1830-40, repeated by simply pulling the trigger, but could not usually be "cocked" as well, the "double action" was the combination of "firing from the trigger" and firing from "full cock," either method being available as preferred.

The Percussion Revolver did invaluable service during the development of the Western States of America and the Australian Colonies, also in the Indian Mutiny and the Crimean War, and its central fire successor is still required wherever the traveller is of necessity his own policeman. It may strike some readers as strange, speaking of the revolver as a valuable instrument in the development of a country. But where all are armed, it makes for law and order, as the majority are generally law abiding, and the turbulent get "short shrift." Mr. Gladstone's friend Prince Nicholas of Montenegro understood this, and at the commencement of his independence when he had little if any standing army, he made an ordinance that every adult male was to carry a revolver, thus placing power to uphold the law in the hands of a peaceably disposed majority, with most satisfactory results in suppressing lawlessness.

In 1858 John Blanch presented a revolver having a detachable butt to Dr. Livingstone, then exploring the Zambesi River, and received the following characteristic letter :—

Private.

My dear Mr. Blanch,

I ought to have written you long ago in acknowledgment of your very kind and truly useful and handsome present. It was not without many a sore tug at my conscience either, but I have been so occupied that I really could not perform that duty. I was provided with a naval officer to assist in the navigation of this river, but the gentleman thinking we could not do without him took on such airs about the position he ought to occupy, though incapable of making the simplest scientific observations, that we were obliged to send him about his business. I then became "skipper" myself, and as we have been furnished with a badly constructed engine, my time has been swallowed up with pursuits I never contemplated on leaving England. These have prevented me from doing my duty to many of my friends at home, some of the hard hearted will never forgive me, but such I conclude you are not, or else you would never have spontaneously served me in the way you have done. I value the revolver very highly, and entreat you to accept my warmest thanks for it, and for the kindly feelings which prompted your generous present.

I have not yet had an opportunity of trying it on game, I have been too much confined to the ship, but I feel sure it will be an exceedingly useful instrument, the stock enables one to take a steady aim, and the size of the ball is sufficient for all small animals. About ten days ago we were up the River Shire 100 miles, and came among enormous herds of elephants on a swampy plain through which the river winds giving off many departing and re-entering branches. We chased some of them with the steamer, and but for an unlucky storm of rain which set in when we caught one in the water we should have secured him ; it was too large of course to try a revolver on, but some weapon of the kind with a larger ball would surely have been very effective. We gave him many shots with the Enfield rifle, then several days afterwards found him lame and plied him with the same but lost him in the storm. Twice we were within fifty yards and were very anxious to have him as fuel for our engine. The plain was 20 or 30 miles broad, and not a tree could be got near the river. The bones of another elephant which the natives had picked clean helped us nicely, hence our desire to get the one referred to. The Shire is deep and well adapted for navigation. We were the first visitors the people ever had, and they seemed very suspicious, but brought fowls, bananas, and cotton yarn for sale. They used bows and poisoned arrows, and only once offered to shoot at us. There was something comical in seeing them place their arrows ready to shoot utterly unconscious of the nature of

F

the arms we carried. We had no encounter—never had and hope we never may—but it is well to be prepared, and thanks to you I am very much so, but still, not so much as to make me in the least desirous of using a weapon against my fellow men. This river is filling now, and a goodly sight it is to see. A large vessel could now, as I stated at home, come up with ease to Tette. I chose the healthy time of the year for coming, though that was not the most favourable for navigation, and you will be glad to hear that my precautions have been completely successful. We have had no fever except among the Kroomen. You may remember the case of the great Niger Expedition, the difference is cause for much thankfulness to the Almighty disposer of events. Please present my kind salutations to your son, and believe

Yours gratefully,
DAVID LIVINGSTONE.

Another French exhibit at the 1851 Exhibition, was by Flobert of Paris, who introduced in 1847, even if he did not invent, the " rim-fire " copper cartridge for pistols and rifles. As the entry in the catalogue says Patented, these were no doubt the well-known saloon pistols and rifles still called by his name. This style of cartridge is the cheapest form of breechloading ammunition, and is annually produced at the present time in hundreds of millions, for miniature rifle shooting. It was developed in size for military arms, and is still in use. It was used in the Peabody, Vetterli, Werndl, Spencer, early Winchester, and many other rifles, and for a long time for revolvers in preference to pin fire, until the central fire cartridge was perfected.

The third and most important foreign invention was the " Needle gun" (group 5, figure 32). This seems to have been shown by several exhibitors. Gehrmann of Berlin, Royal Gun Manufactory of Oberndorf, and Doutrewe of Liège. This celebrated gun or rather rifle was invented by Dreyse of Sommerda, Germany, in 1838, and was partially adopted by Prussia in 1842. The firm of Dreyse

50

51

52

53

54

55

56

57

...LL (U.S.A.) FLINT LOCK BREECHLOADER (1811).
...BERTS BREECHLOADER (1867).
...ABODY (U.S.A.) BREECHLOADER (1862). THE SECOND FORM WITH
HAMMER; THE ORIGINAL FORM WAS HAMMERLESS.
...NEY-WALKER BREECHLOADER (1868).

54. WESTLEY-RICHARDS BREECHLOADER (1869).
55. STEYR (AUSTRIAN SMALL ARMS CO.) BREECHLOADER (1885).
56. ENFIELD, CONVERTED TO NEEDLE-FIRE, BREECHLOADER (1869).
57. LARSEN, DRAMMEN, NORWAY (1842), CAPPING BREECHLOADER, LOADING
INTO BLOCK AND CAPPING UNDERNEATH.

and Collenbush, of Sommerda are among the exhibitors, but only showing percussion caps, so that we may conclude that the inventor was a percussion powder and cap maker, rather than a gunsmith. The term Needle gun had been previously used, and an English patent in 1831 by Moset, describes a Needle gun. Various attempts had been previously made to combine a cartridge with its own means of ignition, notably by Pauly of Paris between 1808 and 1812, as previously mentioned, but here at any rate was a practicable invention, adopted with commendable promptitude by a European Army, and bound to excite the interest of all Governments, and everyone interested in fire-arms. Although the system of this rifle with its " door-bolt " action was destined to develop into the general type of military rifle of the present day, it was not until after 1866, when opposed to the Austrian muzzleloaders, it showed such marked advantages, that it was even admitted that breechloaders must be generally adopted throughout the armies of the world.

Lieutenant C. M. Wilcox, U.S.A., in "Rifles and Rifle Practice," 1859, says :—" In Prussia, part of the infantry is armed with the needle breechloading rifle ; in Sweden and Norway the breechloader is partially introduced : and in France the Cent Guards are so armed. With the above exceptions, no breechloading rifles are in the hands of European troops." And again, " the future will determine whether or not the breechloading arm is to be more generally introduced into service, or to be abandoned."

In its earlier forms the Needle rifle had many defects to set against the quickness with which it could be loaded and fired. As it was not provided with a gastight cartridge, until long afterwards, the escape at the breech after a little use was quite alarming, so much so that soldiers were sometimes afraid to fire them from the shoulder at all, and fired from the hip for fear of damaging their eyes. The cartridge consisted of a bullet having a wad of papier maché at the base of it, in the centre of which towards the powder was the detonating composition ; behind this was the powder enclosed in paper, and there was no thick wad behind the powder to form a gas check, as the needle which came out from the bolt about three-quarters of an inch, had to pass right through the paper and powder before it could reach the detonator. The needle was thus exposed to the heat and corrosion arising from the combustion of the powder. With slight modifications this rifle remained in the German service until after the Franco-German War of 1870, where it was opposed by the " Chassepot," a rifle founded on the same general plan, but modelled in 1866, which had the cap at the back of the cartridge in the middle of a wad, the cap being turned with the hollow to the rear for the needle to strike into, but which was still not a gastight cartridge. The bolt head entered some distance into the chamber, and had a metal shield behind which was a thick wad of india rubber to act as an obturator. In 1871, the Needle rifle was superseded by the Mauser (group 12, fig. 91), which was obviously founded upon it, but which used a solid drawn brass gas-tight cartridge.

No. 158, in the Belgian Section of the 1851 Exhibition, three Infantry guns, Montigny system, was another variation of the Needle gun, of which we give an illustration as a double gun. This was patented in 1849, by the Comte de Chatauvillar (group 1, fig. 5). The essential feature of the action is the employment of a " toggle " joint to the sliding breech piece, and although very unsuited in this form to a sporting gun, it has since been employed in some of the most successful machine guns, repeating rifles, and automatic pistols. Another modification by the same inventor is shown in the sliding barrel action of the Bastin-Lepage gun (group 15, fig. 111). This is of later date and has been considerably used on the continent. The great advantages of a breechloading gastight cartridge are well summarised by Mr. W. W. Greener in his well-known book, "The Gun and its Development," eighth edition 1907, page 127, as follows:—"The essential feature of the modern principle of breech-loading is the prevention of all escape of gas at the breech when the gun is fired by the employment of an expansive cartridge case containing its own means of ignition. In the earlier breechloaders there was an escape of gas through the joints of the mechanism, however well fitted, because the metal expanded at the moment of firing, and the cartridges were formed of a consumable case, or the load was put in a strong non-expansive breech-plug. In those arms in which the ignition was by cap, or other flash from the outside of the barrel, there was, of course, always a considerable escape back through the vent or touch hole in addition. In the earliest efficient modern cartridge case—the pin fire—the cap or detonator is placed within the case ; an anvil, or striking pin, projects through the rim of the case, and, when struck by the hammer, explodes the priming and ignites the charge of powder. The thin weak shell is then expanded by the force of the explosion, until it fits perfectly in the barrel, bears hard against the standing breech, closes tightly round the striking pin, and thus forms a complete and efficient gas check. Further, the cartridge case is a fresh lining to the breech, every shot forming, as it were, a second breech, which relieves the permanent breech of much wear, and prevents its corrosion." This may seem quite obvious now, but it took just forty years after the introduction of the detonating system to find out its advantages and how to obtain them.

The characteristic conservatism of the British War Office is well shown in their refusal for many years, from about 1842, when the Needle rifle was adopted by Prussia, to 1864, to accept any cartridge containing its own means of ignition, that is, a percussion cap of some sort, attached to the cartridge, for service use. Consequently, inventors in this country wasted much valuable energy in the abortive attempt to produce a satisfactory breechloader to be fired by a cap placed outside the barrel, as in a muzzleloader. Our collections offer a bewildering variety of these systems, of which examples will be found in our illustrations. (Group 4, fig. 19, 20; group 5, fig. 27, 28, 29, 30; group 6, fig. 34; group 7, fig. 49; group 8, fig. 57; group 9, fig. 65; group 10, fig. 67; group 11, fig. 75, 76, 77; group 12, fig. 85, 86, 87, 88.)

Almost every imaginable hinged and sliding block system was tried with the capping breechloader, also several forms of the "door bolt" system, two of the latter, Terry's in 1853, and Prince's in 1858, also Westley Richards' hinged block to lift up, in 1858, achieved a considerable success as sporting and target rifles. Both Terry's and Westley Richards' were provisionally issued to some Cavalry Regiments, an unusual honour, which was shared in by Sharp's U.S.A., 1848, and 2,000 by Greene, U.S.A., 1854, were purchased but never issued. (Group 5, fig. 30; group 10, fig. 67; group 6, fig. 34, 38; group 11, fig. 81; group 4, fig. 19, 20.)

The Terry rifle appears to be the first bolt action to have

symmetrical lugs, but they were placed close to the rear end of the bolt; the cartridge had a thick felt wad at the base, which was pushed forward by the bullet of the next cartridge after firing, and a very close joint was effected. The ball for this rifle was larger than the bore, into which it was forced on firing.

The Westley Richards action had the advantage of a projecting neck, which entered the barrel for a short distance beyond the hinge, on the top of the breech end; this also with a thick felt wad in front, effected a very good joint. This rifle had a much more extensive and lengthy term of service than any of the others, being highly approved in South Africa, where it was used for many years, and in fact has only recently been laid aside.

Sharp's rifle was originally fitted with the Maynard continuous primer, had the falling block action with under lever, and was extensively used in America. There is a sentimental connection between this rifle and the well-known plantation melody :—

> "John Brown's body lies mouldering in the ground,
> But his soul goes marching on."

"The celebrated John Brown employed this rifle with great effect against the border ruffians of Missouri. At that time he and a number of Northern men were attempting to make the territory of Arkansas a free state, while Missourians were equally determined to make it a slave state. John Brown, after having two sons assassinated, procured a supply of Sharp's rifles. On one occasion when a troop of about one hundred border ruffians were making a raid into the territory for the avowed purpose of carrying off John Brown, dead or alive, he laid in ambush for them with four Sharp's rifles and four men to load. When they had reached a position on a plain about 400 to 500 yards distant, he opened fire and before they could escape he had killed over twenty of them." John Brown was after all captured by State troops sent against him, tried for conspiracy, and together with four of his sons, hanged in 1859.

Prince's rifle (group 10, fig. 67) was certainly one of the best capping breechloaders. It was constructed on the "door-bolt" principle, but the barrel turned to unlock the breech, and then travelled forward by means of a handle attached to it working in a slot under the stock, the conical breech piece with the lugs on it remaining fast to the stock. With this rifle six shots were fired in 46 seconds, against the Terry rifle, which took one minute four seconds; and on another occasion at Hythe, 120 rounds were fired in 18 minutes. This rifle was highly approved by the trade, and received a testimonial from thirteen London Gunmakers. After quoting this, *The Field*, April 24th, 1858, adds :—" The above reflects great credit on the names attached, showing that they are above the petty jealousies of trade when a question of importance to our national welfare is raised. Indeed, if such an arm was a feature in every household, we might laugh to scorn any landing on our island, even if the whole world was combined against us." These three rifles, Terry's, Westley Richards', and Prince's, probably represent the best that could be done with the system of capping breech-loader, and required to be very well made, as these were, to do it.

One other form of transition breechloader should be mentioned. This was Maynard's, U.S.A., 1851-9, the cartridge of which was of brass with a wide rim for extraction, but did not contain the cap, which was still placed outside the barrel (group 12, fig. 88). This cartridge had a hole at the back, through which the flash could penetrate.

GROUP IX.

58

59

60

61

62

63

64

65

66

ESTELL BREECHLOADER (1871). HAMMER CONNECTED TO BLOCK.
ESTELL BREECHLOADER (1871). HAMMER AND BLOCK SEPARATE.
DOUBLE-HINGED BLOCK BREECHLOADER.
TARR (U.S.A.) BREECHLOADER (1858).
EMINGTON (U.S.A.) BREECHLOADER (1873).

63. WERNDL (AUSTRIA) BREECHLOADER (1867).
64. WESTLEY-RICHARDS BREECHLOADER (1872).
65. GREENE (U.S.A.) BREECHLOADER (1854). FITTED WITH MAYNARD'S
    PRIMER OF 1845.
66. KRUTZSCH BREECHLOADER (1866).

In 1864 the War Office decided upon the adoption of a breech-loading rifle and cartridge containing its own means of ignition. A committee was appointed, and designs called for, suitable for converting the large stock of Enfield rifles and a suitable cartridge for it. About fifty systems were submitted, most of them making use of the original hammer and lock, which were the perfected product of two hundred years. In 1865 the Snider hinged block was selected for adoption, the invention of Jacob Snider, an American, and was issued in 1867, and proved itself a most serviceable design (group 3, fig. 15). The bullet had a hollow base, but without a plug in it, and there was another hollow in the head of it, but the lead was spun over it, so that it was not visible, unless a section was cut out of it. This was a device of Mr. Metford's, and gave greater steadiness in flight, for which he designed it, and also great expansion on impact. Few of the users knew of the use or even the existence of this hollow. The Snider system was avowedly adopted as a temporary expedient, to obtain a quick supply of breechloading rifles, and to use up the large supply of the excellently made Enfield rifles recently constructed.

The central fire gastight cartridge adopted with the Snider rifle was developed as follows. Almost immediately after the pin fire was an established success, further improvements were attempted, and about 1852 Charles Lancaster introduced a central fire gun firing a gastight cartridge. This cartridge was formed with a metal plate in the base, having holes communicating with the powder, and on the back of the plate in the centre was placed the detonating priming. This was covered over the end and a short distance up the side of the cartridge with a copper capsule, on which was formed the rim by which the fired case could be withdrawn by an extractor. This, the first successful central fire, in a few years demonstrated the undoubted advantages of the system ; a cartridge which was symmetrical and easy to handle, and which could be placed quickly in the barrel and the gun closed, without the trouble of fitting the pin into the groove in the barrel, as in the pin fire gun.

An improved form of central fire cartridge was introduced by Daw in 1861, patented by F. E. Schneider, of Paris, which was constructed with an ordinary copper cap placed in the centre of the base, in a metal cup or cap chamber, formed like a slightly larger cap placed over its open end, having a flange which rested inside the base of the cartridge, and a flash hole towards the powder, and inside the cap was placed a metal wedge or anvil, against which the detonating composition in the bottom of the cap was pressed when struck by the firing pin. This cartridge was submitted to the Government for use in rifles, and received an award of (I think) £400, and, in a modified form patented by Colonel Boxer of the Woolwich Staff, with a solid iron rim, but still containing the cap chamber and anvil, was adopted for the Snider rifle. The cap chamber was now made with the flange turned over outside the base of the cartridge. In 1866 Messrs. Eley patented a central fire cartridge, with two anvil, in the cap, a method employed by them for many years, though they have since returned to the single anvil. About this time in a legal action between Daw and Messrs. Eley, the detailed evidence in which I have not read, it was decided that the Schneider patent was not a master patent, and so the manufacture of the central fire cartridge, with slight variations, became general. It would be interesting to know to whom credit is due, if not to Schneider, for the cap chamber and anvil, which first perfected the central fire gastight

cartridge, both for shot guns and rifles.   The solid drawn brass cartridge, with a thick metal base, and an anvil stamped up out of the
solid metal, in the depression forming the cap chamber, is now the latest
development for rifle cartridges.   A committee appointed in 1866 to
consider the most desirable system to adopt for a new rifle, recom-
mended in 1867 a calibre of .450 inch with the barrel rifled on
Henry's (of Edinburgh) system, and the hammerless hinged block
action of Martini.   This rifle known as the Martini-Henry was first
experimentally issued in 1869.   The Martini action, patented in 1868,
was very similar to the original Peabody patented in America in 1862
by Henry O. Peabody, of Boston, Mass.   This was of the hammerless type, of most original design, and one of the greatest simplifica-
tions of a gun action ever invented.   Besides the Martini, which is
described by its inventor in his specification as "an improvement on
the Peabody," the later Westley Richards, Tranter, Swinburn, and
other falling block actions were founded upon it, and it undoubtedly
led up to the modern Anson and Deeley hammerless gun.   However,
owing to the criticism of various authorities, attached by long
usage to the hammer operated by the thumb, with its safety half cock
position, and who were loth to give it up, the inventor was induced
to modify it, by combining a striker coming out on top of the block
at the side, for use with a rim fire cartridge, and the ordinary lock
and outside hammer, in which form the Peabody rifle was adopted by
some of the Armies in Eastern Europe, while Switzerland and
Turkey adopted the original hammerless form, in which the extraction was particularly good compared to the Martini.   The Martini was
in some respects no doubt an improvement upon the Peabody, and
this well known rifle remained in the British service from 1869 to 1888.

Although the Martini (group 3, fig. 16) was selected for the service out of about a hundred and fifty competitors, responding to a War Office circular of 1866, and has proved a very reliable system on the whole, for a single loading rifle, there are two principal objections to it; that the cartridge must be pushed right into the chamber before the block can be closed, and the rather weak extraction, which depends on one movement, there being no primary extraction or cam movement, in both of which respects it is inferior to a bolt action. It is probably also slightly inferior in rapidity. One of its would-be rivals, the second Soper (group 7, fig. 48, and group 11, fig. 83) had an extraordinary superiority in this respect, but an earlier model by the same inventor was rejected in 1866 as being "too complicated, and the safety bolt in the trigger guard not being a sufficient substitute for the half cock." At the competition in 1868 it arrived a day too late, and took no part in the trials, which resulted in the adoption of the Martini.

The wonderful rapidity of the Soper rifle was described in the *Daily Telegraph*, July 18th, 1871:—

"Colonel Fletcher had been explaining to Prince Oscar (of Sweden), the mechanism of the Martini-Henry, and for the purpose of witnessing its effect on the target an adjournment took place to the targets, which Prince Arthur had just quitted. Here the able services of Sergeant Andrews were again requisitioned, and using a ·577 bore Rifle fitted with the Martini action, he got off in three minutes 62 rounds, scoring 2 eyes, 16 centres, and 29 outers; total 114 points. Both Princes were evidently impressed by the performance; but while they were examining and admiring the mechanism of a new rifle by Henry of Edinburgh, in which the breech block contains the lock, and the operation of cocking and ejecting the empty case are effected by a single movement, and of the excellent rifle of Westley Richards, Private Warwick, of the 1st Berks appeared on the scene with the Soper Rifle, an arm which has the reputation as being susceptible of the most rapid manipulation of any which has been invented. In this instance it certainly bore out its reputation, for firing in his peculiar position lying on his back, the sling of the rifle round his right leg, the left foot under the right calf, and tightening the sling, the butt under the right armpit, and the barrel resting in the angle formed by the legs being crossed, Private Warwick worked with a regularity and rapidity suggestive of a human mitrailleuse, getting off in two minutes 68 rounds, and scoring 1 eye, 18 centres, and 33 outers, or a total of 124 points. Such was the rapidity of the firing, that the smoke hung in so dense a cloud at the muzzle of the rifle as to obscure the target, or so excellent a shot would not have made 16 misses at 200 yards. Prince Oscar was warm in his expression of admiration, and said that he had never before seen anything like it."

It will be seen that the Soper fired 68 shots in two minutes, to 62 fired by the Martini in three minutes, or about 60 % faster. *The Field*, April 16th, 1870, stated " that it was actually fired 60 times in one minute, by Private Warwick, 1st Berks, both at the Basing-stoke Exhibition, and since that time in our own presence." At this same Wimbledon Meeting, in the rapid firing contest for teams of four a side, the Soper scored 770 against 306 made by a team armed with Sniders, the Martini not yet being available for Volunteers.

It was during the Martini period that two memorable defeats were suffered by British troops, Laing's Nek, and Majuba Hill, defeats not in any way due to inferiority in the weapons used, but partly attribut-able to the supreme imbecility of taking men into action in white pipe-clayed helmets, and principally to the greatly superior marksmanship and field-craft of the Boers.

The first may be briefly summarised in the following :—" Telegram from the General Officer Commanding Natal and Transvaal, to the Secretary of State for War.

" *January 28, 1881.*

" Moved out with 870 infantry of 58th, 60th, and Naval Brigade; 170 mounted troops and six guns. Main attack was made on spur on left of enemy's position by five companies 58th, supported by mounted troops and artillery.

" 58th was checked by heavy fire at steep shoulder of ridge, and after a gallant and nearly successful charge, in which Colonel Deane, commanding the attack, and all staff and mounted officers were shot down, were driven downhill. Flank charge of mounted troops also repulsed by heavy fire."

G

On January 30. Same to Same.

"Except the loss of many good officers and men and the possible delay in the relief of the Transvaal garrisons, the effects of the check are not serious. The men are in excellent spirits and eager to advance."

The Cape Town correspondent of *The Times*, telegraphed February 2nd, 1881 :—

"The reverse suffered by the troops at Laing's Neck has not occasioned surprise, as the odds were greatly against the small column which was trying to force the precipitous Pass of the Drakensburg."

The result of the defeat as far as the troops were concerned may be realized by a phrase taken from a report in *The Mercury*.

"Sub-Lieutenant Jopp now commands the 58th Regiment."

Majuba followed on February 27th, 1881, and the following account by the special correspondent of *The Standard* is taken from that paper for March 30th, 1881.

MAJUBA HILL.

––––––

Extract from THE STANDARD, *March 30th, 1881.*

MOUNT PROSPECT, *March 4.*

"To chronicle faithfully, accurately,, and without exaggeration, the events of a battle while the narrator still labours under the excitement which inevitably attends a defeat, requires a mind more than ordinarily well balanced. Accordingly, although I trust that the telegrams sent to *The Standard* described faithfully the disastrous fight on Majuba Hill, I have deemed it necessary to allow a day or two to elapse before writing. I have thus been enabled to supplement my own experience by that of others who were in various parts of the battle, and have thus, I hope, rendered my narrative as complete and as accurate as possible. Some terribly fallacious accounts of the fight are flying about camp, and finding credence. Men even who were present advance statements so utterly at variance with what we know to have occured, that great care is necessary in committing anything to paper, especially as it is certain that many of these wild stories are being sent to England as genuine news. With regard to what follows here, I can only say that every incident has been confirmed in two or three different quarters.

" On the night of the 26th, the 'last post' had just gone. Most of our little parties in camp had broken up preparatory to turning in before the 'lights out' bugle, due half an hour later, sounded, when Colonel Stewart, chief of General Colley's staff, looked in at my tent, and quietly cautioned me to be in readiness to turn out; to put on a good pair of walking boots; to have my horse saddled and not to ask questions. Later on I learned that the General, who for some time past had observed that the high and apparently inaccessible peak which overlooks the right of the enemy's position, although held during the day by a Boer picket, was left unoccupied at night, had determined to seize and hold the point at once, fearing that if he delayed any longer the enemy might also discover its value, and entrench it as they had done the Nek. Boer working parties had been seen in close proximity to the top during the day; so to make possession a certainty, the order was given for 180 Highlanders, 148 men of the 58th, 150 Rifles, and 70 Blue Jackets to assemble at 9.30 the same night. I learn that General Colley, feeling himself assured of success, wished that every regiment in his camp might have a share in the victory he expected to win. He hoped that the 58th would wipe out Laing's Nek, and the Rifles the Ingogo. Thus was it that our little force, which together did not equal one regiment in strength, was composed of detachments from four. The General himself told me ' I mean to take the hill, and hold it until the reinforcements come up. Should the enemy endeavour to cut me off, the 2-60th and the Hussars are within call at Newcastle. We are taking three days' rations with us, and before these are finished we ought to be thoroughly secure.' Nevertheless, I for one, as the column moved out, felt that the enterprise on which we were bound was somewhat desperate. The troops marched off from the rendezvous in front of the General's tent at the appointed hour in dead silence. Orders were given in whispers, and as the night was darker than usual, we felt confident of reaching our destination unobserved by the enemy. Soon after leaving camp, we began to ascend the steep slope of a spur which juts out from the main mountain, the long snake-like column looking in the night like a streak of denser darkness. As yet, besides the few in the General's confidence, no one knew what was the object in view; but I have noticed in this war that the soldiers are generally pleased with night marches, feeling that by their means chiefly can we hope to obtain some advantage over our formidable enemy. So all toiled cheerfully upwards, frequent halts giving the panting men time to recover, and even to snatch a few occasional moments of sleep. In two hours we had surmounted the first spur, some fifteen hundred feet above the point from which we started. Here two companies of the Rifles were left behind, with orders to entrench themselves and keep open our communications. The remainder moved along the narrow ridge connecting the lower spur already surmounted with the higher peak overlooking Laing's Nek, for which we were bound.

"Far below us in the enemy's lines we could see an immense fire burning, with numbers of men flitting across the red glare of the flames, and many were the speculatations which were indulged in as to the surprise which awaited 'those festive Boers in the morning.' The footpath on the ridge was narrow; on one side was a deep precipice, on the other an impassable wall of rock and as only one man could move along at a time, it was nearly three in the morning before the column was ready to begin the ascent of the final peak. On the plateau underneath, two more companies were left, one of the 60th and one of the Highlanders, with orders that they also should entrench themselves. Our first attempt to ascend the peak was a failure. We were stopped by an impenetrable mass of bush; but after a time our Zulu guides managed to clamber up a gulley on the left that led to the summit. We followed them, pulling ourselves by our hands over huge boulders and up almost impossible slopes. The first dozen of us who arrived on the top were taken cautiously forward by Colonel Stewart to reconnoitre. We found ourselves on a spacious plateau some thousand yards round, sloping gently downwards from the summit, where was an oblong hollow basin, about two hundred yards long by sixty wide, the ridges of which, as it seemed to us, constituted a natural citadel that we fancied would prove impregnable. There were no signs of the enemy; all was still, and, so far, the expedition promised to turn out a complete success. I was beside the General when he passed the word down for all the troops to come up. Although quiet and self-possessed, I still fancied that in his anxious and careworn countenance there were traces of deep, although suppressed, excitement. It was twenty minutes to four when the first men emerged on the top of the mountain, but before the last had clambered up it was nearly five o'clock. In the interval those of us· who were first up lay down in the grass to snatch a half-hour's sleep. On awakening, a streak of grey light over the hills across the Buffalo River indicated the approach of day, and down two thousand feet beneath us, and behind the Nek, we could see the lights of the Boer encampments twinkling like will-o'-the-wisps, as our enemies, one after the other, lit the fires for their morning coffee—between five and six. As the morning grew older, the Staff were busy posting the men all round the plateau just above where the steep descent began. On one side the hill seemed altogether impracticable; on the other side it was apparently nearly so, although the Boers afterwards found an easy way up. As the day dawned we saw what a splendid position we had gained. The most formidable of the entrenchments on the Nek were not more than two thousand yards distant, and with the Gatling gun, which we had sent for, would be altogether untenable. Many regrets were expressed that our force was not a thousand instead of three-hundred-and-fifty strong, as it seemed but an easy task to steal down the hill-side and surprise the encampment before the enemy had time to realise his danger.

67. PRINCE CAPPING BREECHLOADER (1858).
68. GREEN BREECHLOADER (1871).
69. BOLT BREECHLOADER WITH SIDE LOCK.
70. WILSON BREECHLOADER (1868).

71. JOSLYN (U.S.A.) BREECHLOADER (1870).
72. PIERI BREECHLOADER, BOLT WITH THUMB TRIGGER ON TOP.
73. CHASSEPOT (FRENCH) BREECHLOADER (1866).
74. GRAS (FRENCH) BREECHLOADER (1874).

" The men were posted at ten paces interval, leaving the Naval Brigade and about fifty of the 58th as a reserve in the centre hollow. Each man built for himself a slight stone defence, and, lying down behind it, awaited events. So confident were we of our ability to hold the hill against any force that might come against us, that it struck me even at the time, that sufficient precautions were not being taken to see that each man was properly posted. Many, for instance, I noticed, were lying down where they could not see more than a dozen yards in front. They were not on the extreme brow of the hill, an error that afterwards proved fatal. On the left, however, was a small conical eminence, from which it was fancied we could enfilade any attempt to storm the main position. We were all parched with thirst, but fortunately Lieutenant MacDonald, of the 92nd, dug a well which struck water. Of ammunition we had only taken 75 rounds per man, but more was expected up during the day, so altogether we felt perfectly secure. By six o'clock the enemy's encampments, formed of waggons, laagers with tents inside, were visible. Boers were moving about in all directions, not having as yet discovered us, and shortly the enemy's videttes began to approach to take up their positions for the day. Some of them were stationed as near as three hundred yards from our men, at whose mercy they were. Then arose the question—shall we fire or not? for no definite order on the subject had been given. The troops, however, did not long resist the temptation, and a few shots aimed fruitlessly at a party of mounted Boers gave the latter the alarm. In a moment wild confusion prevailed in their camp. Hundreds of men rushed quickly up and manned the entrenchment on the Nek, others proceeded to drive in their horses and cattle, while a number came galloping round the bottom of the hill, regardless of the smart fire which was opened upon them, and dismounting out of sight, returned us shot for shot. It was then that the question of ammunition forced itself upon the General's notice, so orders were passed round the line to stop all firing, except when the enemy attempted to come within practicable range. During the next hour we saw wave after wave of their skirmishers pass round to the left face of the hill and disappear underneath its slope ; but until nine o'clock, beyond the occasional whiz of a bullet overhead, there was nothing to show that they intended to contest our possession of the position. At that hour, however, a hot fire was opened on part of the hill held by twenty men of the 92nd. The range was soon ascertained by both parties to be 630 yards, and so accurate was the Boers' shooting that every bullet struck the stones behind which our men were lying. These soldiers behaved very steadily, and, mindful of orders, contented themselves by delivering occasional volleys when any of the Boers beneath them showed themselves. Some seven or eight of the latter were reported as hit, while until twelve o'clock only four of our men were slightly wounded. At eleven o'clock, however, Lieut. Hamilton, of the 92nd, who was in command at the point threatened by the enemy, came up to the

General to report that he suspected the Boers to be assembling in strength underneath the steep slope in front of his position, where, of course, they were out of sight. He was offered a reinforcement of twenty men, but took only half-a-dozen, with which he succeeded in checking the enemy's fire. Shortly after eleven, the General, with his Staff, and Commander Romilly, of the Naval Brigade, had been standing upon a part of the plateau on which hitherto the enemy had not aimed any fire. I myself was approaching the part, when my attention was arrested by a puff of smoke from a clump of bushes about nine hundred yards down the hill. A second after, a sharp cry from the General's group showed that the shot had taken effect, and Commander Romilly was seen to roll over and over, mortally wounded, as the doctors afterwards told us. The incident was in full view of almost every man in the force, and I fancy it must have had a bad effect upon our younger soldiers, who saw that to be exposed to the Boer marksmen at almost any range was to court certain death.

" Until twelve, however, the Boer fire, although exceedingly heavy, did little or no damage, and as, down in the enemy's lines, we could see them inspanning their waggons preparatory to trekking away, we began to talk of obtaining possession of the Nek in the morning. We had been exposed to five hours' of unceasing fire, and had become accustomed to the constant humming of bullets, which at noon almost ceased, when the General, wearied with the exertions of the previous night, lay down to sleep. Communication by heliograph had been established with the camp, and confidence in our ability to hold our own had increased, rather than abated. Lieutenant Hamilton, however, who, with his few men, had been opposing the enemy alone throughout the morning, without even receiving a visit from the General or his Staff, did not share in the general assurance. A little after twelve he came back from his position for a few minutes to tell us that, having seen large numbers of the enemy pass to the hollow underneath him, he feared that they were up to some devilment. Reinforcements were promised him and he returned to his post, but these, as I now know, did not reach him until it was almost too late. Shortly afterwards, Major Hay, of the 92nd, Colonel Stewart, Major Fraser, and myself, were discussing the situation. The former expressed an opinion that we were not strong enough to repulse a night attack. I had remarked that the Boers would probably make their final effort at about four in the evening, as they did at the Ingogo, when we were startled by a loud and sustained rattle of musketry, the bullets of which shrieked over our heads in a perfect hail. Lieutenant Wright, of the 92nd, rushed back, shouting out for immediate reinforcements. The General, startled up from his sleep, assisted by his Staff, set about getting these forward, and then for the first time it dawned upon us that we might lose the hill, for the soldiers moved forward but slowly and hesitatingly. It was only too evident they did not like the work before them. By dint of some hard shouting and even pushing, they were most of them got over the ridge, where they lay down, some distance behind Hamilton and his thin line of Highlanders, who, although opposed to about five hundred men at one hundred and twenty yards, had never budged an inch. It seems that the advance of the enemy had been thoroughly checked, when one of our people—an officer I believe—noticing the Boers for the first time, ejaculated, 'Oh, there they are, quite close;' and the words were hardly out of his lips ere every man of the newly-arrived reinforcements, bolted back panic-stricken. This was more than flesh and blood could stand, and the skirmishing line under Hamilton gave way also, the retreating troops being exposed, of course, to the Boer fire with disastrous effect. I was on the left of the ridge when the men came back on us, and was a witness of the wild confusion which then prevailed. I saw MacDonald, of the 92nd, revolver in hand, threaten to shoot any man who passed him; and, indeed, everybody was hard at work rallying the broken troops. Many, of course, got away, and disappeared over the side of the hill next the camp, but some hundred and fifty good men, mostly Highlanders, blue jackets, and old soldiers of the 58th, remained to man the ridge for a final stand. Some of the Boers appeared, and the fire that was interchanged was something awful. Three times they showed themselves, and three times they as quickly withdrew, our men, when that occurred, at once stopping their fire. I could hear the soldiers ejaculate, 'We'll not budge from this. We'll give them the bayonet if they come closer,' and so on; but all the time dropping fast, for Boer marksmen had apparently got to work in secure positions, and every shot told, the men falling back hit, mostly through the head. Colour-Sergeant Fraser, of the 92nd, one of the finest soldiers in the corps, dropped close to me with both legs shattered to pieces, and many others of his Regiment, whom I had known in Afghanistan, met a similar fate, just as their days of soldiering were drawing to an honourable close.

" Altogether it was a hot five minutes, but nevertheless I personally thought at the time we should hold our own. I expected every minute to hear the order given for a bayonet charge. That order unfortunately never came, although I am sure the men would have responded to it. But our flanks were exposed, and the enemy, checked in front, were stealing round them; across the hollow on the side of the hill facing camp we had no one, and as the men were evidently anxious about that point, frequently looking over their shoulders, Colonel Stewart sent me over to see how matters were going on. There I reported all clear, and, indeed, if the enemy had attempted to storm the hill on that face he would have been decimated by the fire of his own people aimed from the other side. We were most anxious about our right flank. It was evident that the enemy were stealing round it, so men were taken to prolong the position there. They were chiefly blue jackets, led by a brave young officer, and, as I watched them follow him up, for the third time that day, the conviction flashed across me that we should lose the hill. There was a knoll on the threatened point, up which the reinforcements hesitated to climb. Some of them went back over the top of the plateau to the further ridge, others went round. Bye-and-bye there was confusion on the knoll itself. Some of the men on it stood up, and were at once shot down; and at last the whole of those who were holding it gave way. Helter skelter they were at once followed by the Boers, who were able then to pour a volley into our flank in the main line, from which instant the hill of Majuba was theirs. It was *sauve qui peut*. Major Hay, Captain Singleton of the 92nd, and some other officers, were the last to leave, and these were immediately shot down and taken prisoners. The General had turned round the last of all to walk after his retreating troops, when he also was shot dead, through the head. A minute or two previously, Lieutenant Hamilton, requesting the General to excuse his presumption, had asked for a charge, as the men would not stand the fire much longer. Colley replied, 'Wait until they come on, we will give them a volley and then charge;' but before that moment arrived it was too late. To move over about one hundred yards of ground under the fire of some five hundred rifles at close range is not a pleasant experience, but it is what all who remained of us on the hill that day had to go through. Every moment I expected to feel a bullet crash through me. Every step I expected would be my last. On every side men were throwing up their arms, and with sharp cries of agony were pitching forward on the ground. A bullet struck the rock at my heel, the splinters hitting my leather leggings, whilst overhead and on either side the missiles shrieked past with the noise of a thousand locomotives. At last I reached the shelter of the further ridge. Colonel Stewart and Lieutenant Hill, of the 58th, being close to me. The latter—who had behaved splendidly during the action—was shot through the arm, and I gave him my handkerchief to bind his wound. The officers were calling out to the men to rally, when a soldier cannoned against me and knocked me into the bushes on the precipice underneath. The Boers were instantly on the ridge above, and for about ten minutes kept up their terrible fire on our soldiers, who plunged down every path. Many, exhausted with the night's marching and the day's fighting, unable to go further, lay down behind rocks and bushes, and were afterwards taken prisoners; but of those who remained on the hill to the very last, probably not one in six got clear away. The period during which I was suspended in the bush at the mercy of the Boers firing only some three or four yards above my head, was, I think, the most unpleasant of the whole day. I did not expect that men in the heat of action would spare me; but they did, and helped me at last, out of my awkward position on to the ridge again. There, after being divested by my captors of spurs, belt, and some money, I demanded to be taken before the General. I was let go, and told to find him myself, and made my way to the hollow where he had passed the day.

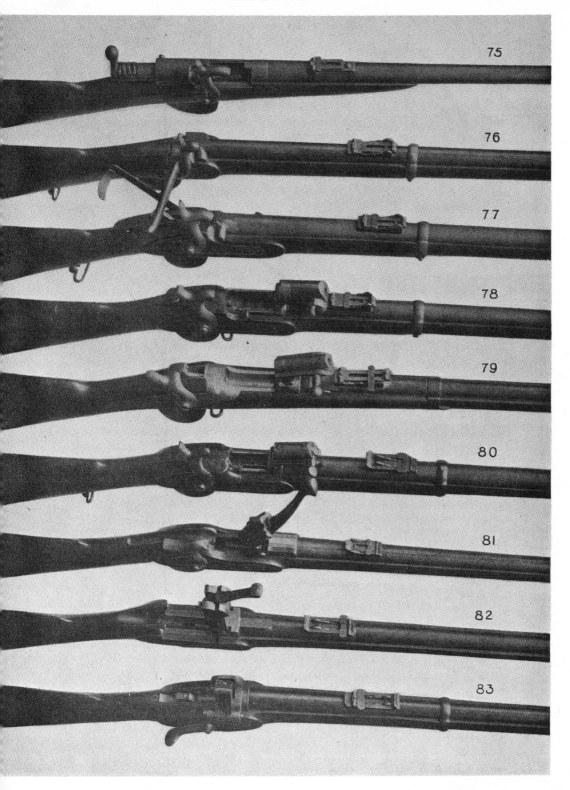

" I there found myself amongst a crowd of Boers, prisoners and wounded, and dying men. There was a group round one body, and I was at once pounced upon to say who it was. I responded, ' General Colley,' but they would hardly believe me. The Boers were everywhere assisting our disabled men. Dr. Landon, who, when the hill was abandoned by our panic-stricken troops, had steadily remained by his wounded, was lying on the ground with a shot through his chest. The Boers as they rushed on the plateau, not seeing or not caring for the Geneva Cross, had fired into and knocked over both him and his hospital assistant, so there was only one, Dr. Mahon, left to look after a great number of very bad cases. After some difficulty I found Smith, the Boer General, and explained to him my business, asking permission to proceed to the British Camp. It was some time before he would allow me to go, as he said that General Joubert would probably like to see me.; but at last I obtained a pass, on condition that I returned next day. I found the Boers everywhere exceedingly civil. Their bearing was manly, without the slightest trace of exultation. They one and all ascribed their victory to the God of Battles, who they said was on their side. Indeed, these men are possessed by much of the spirit which actuated the Covenanters of Scotland in the last generation, and it is a spirit which urges on men, whether they be Christians or Mussulmans, Boers or British, to fight desperately and valorously. As my guides conducted me down the hill outside the line of their sentries, we witnessed the Boer attack on the laager where General Colley had posted a company of Highlanders and one of Rifles. It did not last long, as our men had received an order from camp by signal to evacuate the position. A troop of Hussars had joined them in the morning, which was to have escorted out some reserve ammunition ; but the ground was too broken for cavalry to act, so all went down the hill together, exposed to a heavy fire. Our loss here was about twenty killed, wounded, and prisoners. The number would have been much greater if the pursuit had not been checked by the guns in camp opening on the Boers, who appear to dislike artillery. Not that the shells did them much damage on this occasion at least, on the contrary, the only result of the fire, so far as I could see, was four or five of our own men placed *hors de combat* by a badly-directed shot. It was nearly six in the evening before I reached camp, where I was astonished to find that hardly any of those who had remained on the hill to the last had preceded me. Only men who had left before the final rush took place had got in, and these, of course, knew but little of what occurred. Colonel Bond, the next senior officer in camp to General Colley, on learning from me of the latter's undoubted death, at once took measures to place the camp in a thorough state of defence. A flag of truce was sent out, with ambulances for the wounded ; but it was dark before Dr. Babbington, who was in charge, could reach the summit of the hill. As after the Ingogo fight, it rained in torrents all night, and the wretched wounded on the hillside must have suffered untold agonies, which indeed, in some instances continued for two days, for the disabled men were scattered over a wide space, many of them lying in dense bush where it was difficult to find them. They are now, however, all well cared for, Dr. McGahan, who remained all night on the Ingogo field, having been sent for from Newcastle to supplement the limited medical staff here. The morning after the field I redeemed my promise of returning to the Boer lines, where I was taken before Mr. Joubert. What I saw there and the substance of my conversation with that celebrated individual must stand over for another letter. Suffice it only to say that from him I received my final discharge.

" Having given above the incidents of the fight as they occurred, it is for your readers to draw their own conclusions as to the causes of the disaster. There can be no doubt that the position was too extended for the number of men defending it, but still the hill is so high, so steep and formidable, that we all, from the General downwards, until the final rush, never dreamt that the Boers would be able to get close enough to put our capacity to hold the peak really to the test. They, however, proceeded methodically to work, and taking their time, were content to ascend some fifty yards only per hour, until finally eventually they took us by surprise. At the last, too, the Boer General, finding that his main position on the Nek was not in danger, detached the bulk of his forces to aid in the assault on the hill, and as they only attacked one point, the Boer fire from first to last mastered ours, in extent no less than in accuracy. At the end our men were uneasy about their flanks. The difficulty in taking aim owing to the danger of exposing oneself even for a second rendered our fire unsteady, and the real fighting instincts of the British soldier were never once roused. When the crisis arrived, too, owing to the mixture of different corps, and to the want of order and system that prevailed, there was a difficulty in moving men to the threatened points. The soldiers were not commanded by their own officers, and consequently there was a want of mutual confidence. I feel certain that if our forces had all been taken from one regiment—say the 92nd—the Boers would have met with a disastrous repulse. With reference to the story that our men fell short of ammunition, I can only say that our firing continued up to the very last, and as to bayonet charges, which failed through the soldiers being shot down, I saw none, nor do I believe that any took place. The General intended beyond doubt to deliver one, but before the opportunity which he awaited for arrived it was too late. Our flank was by that time turned, and the day was lost."

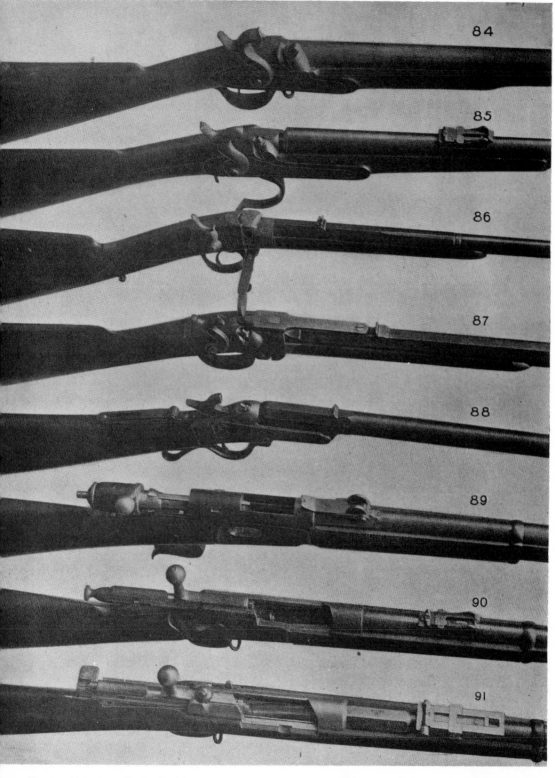

84

85

86

87

88

89

90

91

STLEY-RICHARDS MUSKET FOR PAPER CAP (1841).
VTON HINGED BARREL CAPPING BREECHLOADER (1855).
WAY REVOLVING-BREECH-BLOCK-CAPPING BREECHLOADER, LOADING
  AND CAPPING IN BLOCK, ON EACH SIDE.
BERT SMITH (U.S.A.) CAPPING BREECHLOADER, HINGED BARREL
  (1857).

88. MAYNARD (U.S.A.) HINGED BARREL CAPPING BREECHLOADER, FOR
    METAL CARTRIDGE (1859).
THREE TUBE-MAGAZINE RIFLES.
89. VETTERLI (SWISS), TUBE UNDER BARREL (1869).
90. HOTCHKISS-WINCHESTER (U.S.A.), TUBE IN STOCK (1875).
91. MAUSER (GERMANY), TUBE UNDER BARREL (1884).

CHAPTER IV.

HAMMERLESS AND EJECTOR GUNS.　　SINGLE-TRIGGERS.
PUMP GUNS.　　THE AUTO-LOADING SYSTEM.

FROM the Hammerless Martini Rifle we may well pass to the Hammerless Sporting Double Gun. In a very few years after the introduction of the central fire cartridge, the manufacture of pin fire guns ceased altogether in this country, although it continued much longer on the continent. We need not describe the various modifications in the action employed in the central fire Hammer Gun, as they are still in use and familiar to sportsmen, but an important departure was made just after the Martini had been introduced, and the original Peabody and other rifles had been designed with the lock-work contained in the breech action, and without an external hammer for the thumb to operate, by Murcott of the Haymarket, who patented his hammerless double gun in 1870, with side locks, and a push down under snap lever. From its strange box-like appearance and the loud noise it made in closing, it was nicknamed, in the trade, " Murcott's Mouse Trap." Earlier attempts to introduce Hammerless Guns had been made, but without success. Needham's in 1850, was without hammers, and Daw offered the Schneider hammerless gun in 1862, about the same time that he introduced his central fire hammer gun and cartridge, which had piston-like locks, and was a modification of the needle gun ; Beckwith also in 1865 offered the Carle hammerless gun of the same type. Hammerless double guns

H

on the needle principle had been made on the continent from 1850-60. The usual remark was that, " they looked like a dog without ears," but the real objection to them was, that they were either without a safety bolt, or it was so placed as to be difficult to handle, consequently, they were more dangerous than hammer guns, as they were always at "full-cock," and a fellow sportsman had not the satisfaction of seeing whether the hammers were half cock, full cock, or down.   In this respect Murcott's was a decided advance, as it had a safety lever moving in an arc on the top of the action, prominently in view and easy to get at.   Although this gun enjoyed only a moderate success, as it was heavy and noisy, a strong lever being used to cock both locks as well as withdraw the bolt, and a strong spring required to return the heavy lever, it marked the turning point, and from this time, the hammerless gun had come to stay.

In 1874, another remarkable gun was patented by Needham. This had the locks mounted on an under frame instead of side plates, was also operated by a push down snap lever, but had the entirely new feature of ejecting the fired cartridge or cartridges, completely away from the gun, when opened after firing.   If not fired, the cartridges were only brought out a short distance as usual.   This gun created a great deal of interest, but was handicapped by requiring an inconvenient amount of force applied to both the lever and the barrels, to cock the locks and operate the ejectors, which were actuated in a most ingenious way from the same mainsprings as the locks.   It was also awkward to mount the barrels on the stock, and rather heavy. However this was the first gun with independent extractors to each barrel, which flicked either or both cartridges clear of the gun, if they had been fired, without handling them.

The next advance was a simplified hammerless gun, which was much easier to open, and much safer to handle, though at first without ejectors.

The Westley Richards falling block rifle, 1868, had the tumbler which also formed the striker, pivotted directly under the breech end of the barrel, and in front and above the tumbler under the barrel was placed the mainspring. This arrangement adapted to a double gun, with the novel feature of connecting the tumblers, by means of the forward extension of them, underneath the mainsprings, with levers operated by the forepart, for re-cocking the locks, was patented by Anson and Deeley and introduced by Westley Richards in 1875, and was improved in 1876, by the addition of the automatic safety on the tang of the action. The special feature of this gun, which constituted a great advance on all previous hammerless guns, was that the locks were cocked by the fall of the barrels, whereby ample leverage was obtained, and the opening and cocking of the gun effected with less effort than in any previous model. The triggers were also automatically locked every time the gun was opened, so that they had to be consciously unlocked, which was effected by an easy movement of the thumb, without shifting the hand. The advantages of this invention were at once appreciated, and in a few years, the side lock gun was modified by various inventors so as to connect the locks with the forepart, and cock the gun by the fall of the barrels, as in the Anson and Deeley. This is now the general system, but the Purdey gun, Beesley's patent, 1880, is a notable exception, as in this the opening removes a cam from the top side of the mainspring, which at once allows this specially shaped spring to throw the tumblers back to full cock, and on closing the barrels the mainsprings are again compressed ready for firing. This is a beautiful mechanism as made by this celebrated maker, but requires unusual accuracy in manufacture and in the harmony of all the parts, and is consequently out of the question for a cheap gun.

Since the establishment of the Hammerless Ejector Double Gun as the leading type of sporting weapon only one noticeable development has achieved any marked success, namely, Single-triggers. The idea of discharging a double gun or pistol by means of a single trigger seems to go back to almost the earliest days of such weapons. A pair of under and over, double barrelled, wheel lock pistols, with single triggers, may be seen in the Wallace Collection in Manchester Square; the exact details of these pistols I do not know, but in a similar lock which I have examined, the two wheels were mounted on the same plate tandem fashion, and the two sears were connected by a slack chain, the trigger bearing against the rear sear first discharged the rear wheel and tightened the chain, and a further pull on the trigger would then discharge the front wheel. These weapons were very heavy holster pistols over a foot long, and used a very small charge in proportion to their weight, so that with care such a crude arrangement might work fairly well, though there was nothing to prevent the discharge of both barrels if the pull on the trigger was too vigorous.

In the later flint lock period many double pistols with both under and over and side by side barrels were made with single triggers. The earliest patent in this country was to James Templeman, of Salisbury, in 1789, " making locks to discharge double barrel guns and pistols by means of one trigger only, without any possibility of

92

93

94

95

96

97

98

99

100

101

DOUBLE PIN-FIRE RIFLE, DISCS SCREWING INTO BARRELS
(GENHART) (1857).
LARSEN BREECHLOADER (DRAMMEN, NORWAY).
HARSTON BREECHLOADER (1871).
WYLEY BREECHLOADER (1871).
WEBLEY-WYLEY BREECHLOADER (1874).

97. HEEREN BREECHLOADER (NAGEL & MENZ, BADEN) (1880).
98. BETHEL BURTON BREECHLOADER (1864-70).
99. BEAUMONT BREECHLOADER (HOLLAND) (1859) MAGAZINE (1891).
100. ORIGINAL LEE-REMINGTON (U.S.A.) MAGAZINE (1879).
101. SAVAGE (U.S.A.) MAGAZINE (1893).

discharging both barrels at the same instant. . . . will completely remove that defect which has attended all other locks yet invented," &c.; showing that other plans had been in use and were defective. The plan he proposed was to fit an extra sear to the left sear, which had to be first disengaged by the trigger before the left sear proper. John Manton, in a patent of 1797 describes flint locks having one "tricker" for discharging two locks. This employed a switching blade, pressed by a spring under the right sear, and forced over to the left on the fall of the right tumbler. H. Nock made some double pistols in which the trigger was under the right sear, but had a hinged piece coming under the left sear, held in position by a spring which gave way while the right barrel was fired, when the hinged piece reached a stop and a further pull fired the left. The right pull was made lighter than the left, but of course, a long, strong pull fired both in rapid succession. D. Egg constructed pistols with a single trigger, fitted rather closer to the right lock than the left, and carrying a see-saw piece which reached under both sears, the left pull being much harder than the right. The right is released first, and on the right tumbler a spring hook is arranged to snap over the sear nose, and hold it fast to the tumbler, so that the tail of the sear forms a steady fulcrum for the see-saw when the trigger is again pressed to discharge the left lock. Jochard, of Paris, made a double pistol with single (secret) trigger, to which two arms were fitted, the right being given a slight lead, so that the right sear was released first if pulled carefully, and a further pull without letting go of the trigger fired the left. If the left is at half cock, no special care is required, and this is probably the way it was intended to be used. Some percussion double pistols with single trigger were made by Rigby, in which a switching trigger blade was positively operated by a zig-zag groove formed around a ratchet operated wheel.

The recent revival of single triggers dates from about 1882, when W. Baker, of Birmingham, began improving them, and has since taken out several patents, the leading principle of which is a sliding piece which travels forward after firing the right lock, but is caught by an interceptor before reaching the position to fire the left lock, the "involuntary pull" on the trigger occasioned by the rebound of the gun from the shoulder, releasing the slide from the interceptor, and allowing it to take up position under the left sear, so that the left lock may be discharged. The same principle, the employment of the involuntary pull or pressure of the finger on the trigger after recoil, is utilized by Messrs. Boss, in their very ingenious and original mechanism, with the additional advantage of positive locking of the left sear while discharging the right. The arrangement which suggests the escapement of a watch, consists of a small turret pivotally mounted on the trigger plate, which can be lifted by the trigger, and which can turn so as to lift either sear alternately, but never both. The turret is impelled by a spring in one direction, and re-set by a rod in the other direction on opening the gun. The right lock being fired, the turret revolves, but is arrested by a step on its coming against the trigger, which must be raised by the involuntary pull before the turret can continue to revolve, and so bring a part under the left sear ready to be discharged by the next pull of the trigger.

Another principle which has been successfully employed is known as a "timer." Messrs. Holland's patent is on this principle, an unusually long slide being employed, impelled by a light spring, the distance to be covered between firing the right and the position for firing the left, occupies sufficient time to render the trigger inoperative to the involuntary pull. Beesley's system employs a timer in the form of a quadrant, which controls the travel of the trigger, and which can be momentarily arrested by the involuntary pull; but until it has completed about a sixth of a circle, will not allow the trigger to reach the left sear. No forward release of the trigger by the finger is necessary with this system, the left sear being slightly higher than the right.

Another highly ingenious mechanism is that of Messrs. Westley-Richards, which may be described as a timer controlled by the recoil by means of an oscillating weight. When the right is fired, the weight rocks forward over its pivot, which is under the impulse of the recoil, and kicks a hooked limb into engagement with a fixed detaining limb, the involuntary pull only tending to more tightly lock them together. Upon the return of the weight to its rear position, even if the involuntary pull has not yet occurred, such a sudden movement will again lock the hook to the detaining piece, but upon the normal pressure of the voluntary pull for the discharge of the second barrel, the hook is first lifted over a check stud on the trigger plate, and the trigger is then free to rise and release the left sear.

Many other systems have been devised and are in successful operation, and something like a hundred patents have been granted on this subject during the last twenty years in this country, but it still seems doubtful if the principle of single triggers for double guns will become generally adopted. In spite of there being many enthusiastic users of single triggers there are several drawbacks to their use which may be stated. In the first place it is obvious that as the finger is already in position for a second discharge immediately after the first, if you only hug the trigger long enough a second discharge will occur. There is time for the gun to rebound several times from the shoulder to the finger, and yet produce successive discharges that appear to the ear to be simultaneous, and a small percentage of individuals seem unable to desist from continuing to press the trigger, and are consequently unable to use a single trigger gun.

Secondly, a certain amount of delicacy is inevitable in the mechanism, however well made and ingenious, as instead of moving the finger, an inside limb must be moved by a spring or other device to make connection between the trigger and the second sear, with which it was not in connection in its first position.

An amount of rust or gummy oil which would be a matter of indifference in a double trigger gun is sufficient to stop the working of most single trigger actions.

Another objection in the case of guns with the left barrel more closely choked than the right, is that the left barrel cannot be used first, unless an additional slide or reversing limb is fitted, which is placed in many cases on the trigger plate inside the guard, or as in Baker's system is operated by pushing the trigger itself forward.

Guns have been constructed in which both barrels could be fired from the front trigger, and a rear trigger was provided for the occasional discharge of the left barrel first. Others have been made in which both barrels could be discharged from either trigger. Some advantages would be offered by the plan of usually discharging both barrels from the rear trigger, and providing a front trigger for

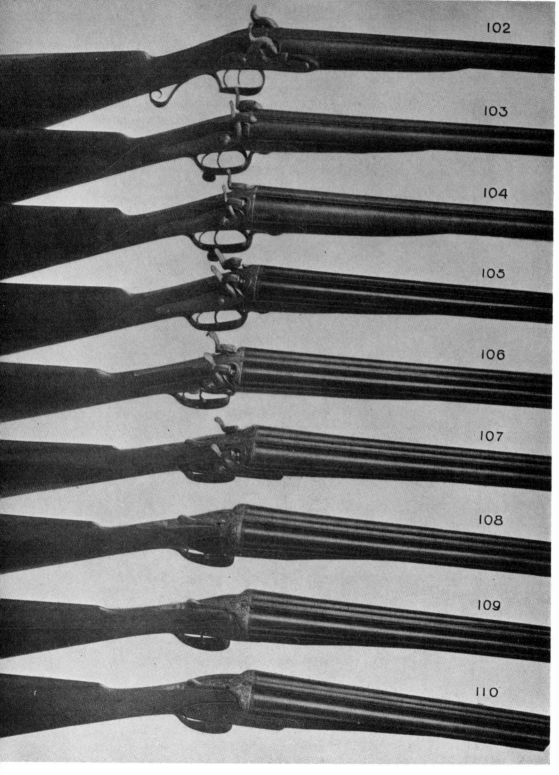

BLANCH GUNS, 1809-1909.

102. FLINT LOCK, CONVERTED TO PERCUSSION, 1809-25.	106. SIDE LEVER (FROM 1872).
103. PIN FIRE BREECHLOADER (FROM 1856). AT FIRST WITH SINGLE GRIP AND STRAIGHT LEVER UNDER FORE-END.	107. TOP LEVER, ALSO AS PIN FIRE (FROM 1869).
104. CENTRAL FIRE, UNDER LEVER DOUBLE GRIP (FROM 1866).	108. HAMMERLESS, ANSON & DEELY (FROM 1878).
105. SNAP UNDER LEVER, ALSO AS PIN FIRE (FROM 1864).	109. HAMMERLESS SIDE LOCKS (FROM 1880).
	110. HAMMERLESS EJECTOR SIDE LOCKS (FROM 1888).

the occasional discharge of the choked barrel first. The hand would then not have to be released when operating the rear trigger, which is the principal advantage offered by any single trigger system.

The development of Repeating Firearms, which on the revolving system had taken such a step forward after the invention of the copper cap, was enabled to take another stride soon after the invention of the copper rim fire cartridge, and before we return to the military rifle we may notice that an entirely new class of Repeating Sporting Guns, to use the ordinary 12-bore paper shot cartridges, were in course of development in America simultaneously with the Ejector Hammerless Gun in England. The first seems to have been the Roper, 1866 ; this had a revolving magazine for four cartridges, and also the curious feature of carrying the cartridge from the magazine as well as firing it, after the trigger was pulled. It was operated entirely by the thumb piece of the hammer (group 18, fig. 127). This system had many defects compared to a double barrelled breechloader, and is only noticeable for its undoubted originality. The Spencer repeating gun of 1882 was a further original development, as the opening, extracting and reloading were effected by a slide, the handle of which formed a forepart and was held in the left hand while firing. This gave, with a little practice, extraordinary rapidity in the dis-charge of its five cartridges, which were contained in a tubular magazine under the barrel. In 1886 the Winchester was introduced, having a right-handed under lever action ; this was succeeded by another Winchester (Browning's) in 1893 with a left-handed slide. Burgess, in 1893, offered a variation in a right-handed slide, fitting round the small of the stock, and Marlin, 1898, and Stevens (Browning's) 1908, have also followed with guns operated like the Spencer. All of these sliding action guns, generically known as Pump Guns, have had an extensive sale in America and the Colonies, though so little has been seen of them in this country, and though capable of wonderful rapidity in the hands of an expert, they do not offer that extreme facility in handling characteristic of the Hammerless Ejector Gun, and require more knack and practice to use effectively.

The latest development in small arms now being applied to Guns, Rifles and Pistols, is a further extension of the repeating principle, and is generally spoken of as the Automatic System, but is more correctly described as the Self-loading or Auto-loading system, as the real Automatic system, which includes the firing as well as reloading of the piece as long as there is a cartridge in the belt or magazine, is strictly applicable only to the Maxim Automatic Machine Gun, from which the principle as far as the reloading is concerned, is adopted.

This marvellous weapon, the invention of Sir Hiram Stevens Maxim, was patented in 1883, and acts as an explosive motor, the force usually expended after the departure of the bullet, in recoiling the piece, being utilized for reloading, and if required maintaining a continuous fire. The barrel and breech piece recoil together for a short distance, the breech is then unlocked and the barrel arrested, the breech piece continuing its travel and drawing out the fired cartridge, which is carried away by a wheel feeder which also brings round a fresh cartridge, which has been drawn out of a belt and placed in the feeder by a previous operation, by hand or firing. Attached to the breech piece by a rod is a crank fixed across the frame of the gun at the back, which carries a " fusee " regulator, by

111. BASTIN-LEPAGE PIN FIRE (PARIS) (ABOUT 1860).
112. NEEDHAM NEEDLE FIRE. NOT A GASTIGHT CARTRIDGE (1852).
113. BACON CENTRAL FIRE GASTIGHT CARTRIDGE (1870).
114. JEFFRIES, OF NORWICH. AS A PIN FIRE (1862).
115. REMINGTON (U.S.A.) HINGED BLOCK DOUBLE GUN (1873).

which a spring is put in tension. Before the crank has completed a full revolution, the spring reacts and returns all the parts to their original position, carrying a new cartridge into the barrel, locking the breech, and if set for continuous firing, discharging the gun, the lock having been re-cocked by the previous backward movement. If set for deliberate fire it can be discharged by a trigger attached to a pistol handle at the back of the gun. The principal advantage of the Maxim over any previous Machine Gun is not so much its increased rate of fire as the absence of the disturbance to the aiming caused by the movement of the crank or lever used in the older hand-operated Machine Guns, such as the Mitrailleuse (1867), Gatling (1869), Gardner (1876), Nordenfelt (1878), and Hotchkiss (1879), which necessitated the clamping of the gun, more or less, during discharge. Owing to the absence of this disturbance the Maxim Gun can be mounted freely on a swivel and pointed in any direction during firing as easily as one can point a fire hose, stops being used to limit the arc of fire when training the gun on distant objects. To illustrate this facility in training the gun, the inventor was in the habit of writing his name on the target with bullet holes when demonstrating its capabilities.

The application of the Auto-loading principle of the Maxim Gun to small arms, but of course without its capacity for continuous fire, is the principal object of attainment before inventors at the present time.

Nearly a hundred years ago a steam gun was constructed by Perkins to discharge balls by means of high pressure steam; of course only very low ballistics were obtained, and the outfit included a boiler and furnace. A demonstration was given before the Duke of Wellington, who, after witnessing it, remarked—"It would be a very good thing if gunpowder had not been invented."

In 1854 Bessemer patented a self-acting breechloader, but not a small arm or what we should now call a machine gun, but rather some sort of cannon I should think, in which the explosion in some way set free some auxiliary apparatus, operated by water, air, or steam, which reloaded and again fired the gun. The possibility of applying the principle of Auto-loading to small arms has been obvious ever since the Maxim Gun appeared, and Sir Hiram has himself applied it to a variety of guns, rifles, and pistols—in fact many of his early experiments were connected with small arms rather than machine guns.

As it is now twenty-five years since these early patents were taken out, the general principle is no longer covered by a master patent, and consequently many attempts are being made to apply the principle of Auto-loading in its various forms to the different classes of small arms for sporting and military purposes. With regard to pistols, considerable success has already been attained, and the Borchardt (1893), Bergmann (1894), Mauser (1896), Maxim (1896), Browning (1897), Browning (1898), Mannlicher (1898), Fairfax (1900), Colt (1903), and Webley (1904), have demonstrated the advantages over the revolver obtainable by the Auto-loading principle. In shot guns the Browning is at present the only one which has been made in large numbers, and owing to its popular price of about ten pounds, may prove a formidable rival to the Hammerless Ejector Gun.

Rifles on this principle may still be considered in the experimental stage, and although Mauser, Mannlicher and Browning have produced designs of the greatest ingenuity, the requirements of a

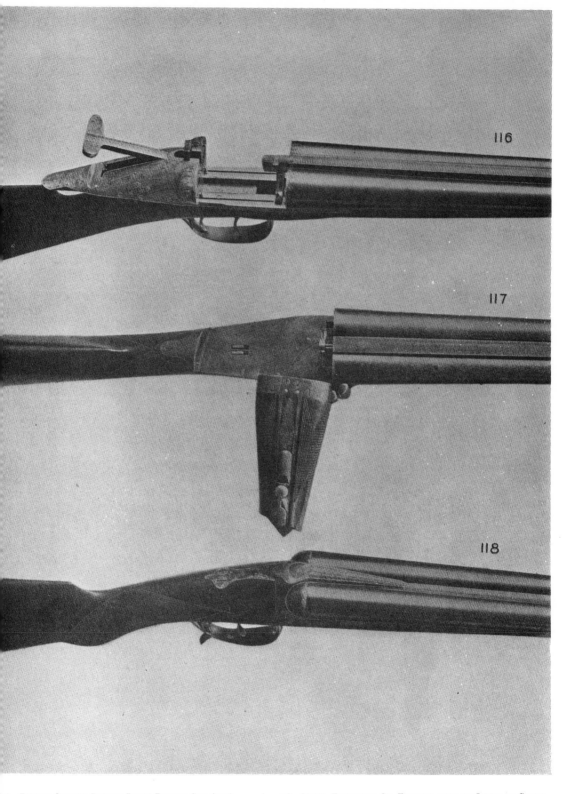

116. FRENCH SLIDING BREECH BLOCK DOUBLE GUN (1909).
117. GYE & MONCRIEFF (1882).

118. MNFR. FRANCAISE, ST. ETIENNE, PULL UP LEVER IN GUARD
BLACHON & MIMARD PATENT (1888).

military or high power sporting rifle have not yet been completely satisfied. There can be no doubt, however, that if a further simplification can be attained, the military powers are fully prepared to adopt them, at least for special corps, the advantage anticipated from such a weapon being not so much dependent upon an increased rapidity of discharge as upon an increased rapidity and economy of effort in aiming, the hands not having to be removed from their hold of the rifle, or the poise of the body disturbed until the magazine requires replenishing.

We will now return to the Military Rifle, which we left at its single loading stage, and describe a few of the first successful types.

CHAPTER V.

Repeating and Magazine Rifles. The Lee-Enfield.

THE idea of a repeating gun is a very old one; even a magazine cross bow is, or was, in the United Service Museum, and attempts have been made for more than two hundred years in this direction, as the following from our old friend Pepys will show:—
"July 3rd, 1662. Dined with the officers of the Ordnance, where Sir W. Compton, Mr. O'Neile, and other great persons were. After dinner, was brought to Sir W. Compton a gun to discharge seven times; the best of all devices that ever I saw, and very serviceable, and not a bauble; for it is much approved of, and many thereof made."

And again—"March 4th, 1664. There were several people trying a new-fashion gun brought my Lord Peterborough this morning, to shoot off often, one after another, without trouble or danger."

Match lock guns have been made similar to the percussion gun illustrated (group 18, fig. 123) with four or more flash holes, but these, I think, generally only contained four charges of powder with wadding between, and the ball had to be added each time. They were very heavy in the barrel in case more than one charge went off at a time, and the slight saving in time in loading was obviously not

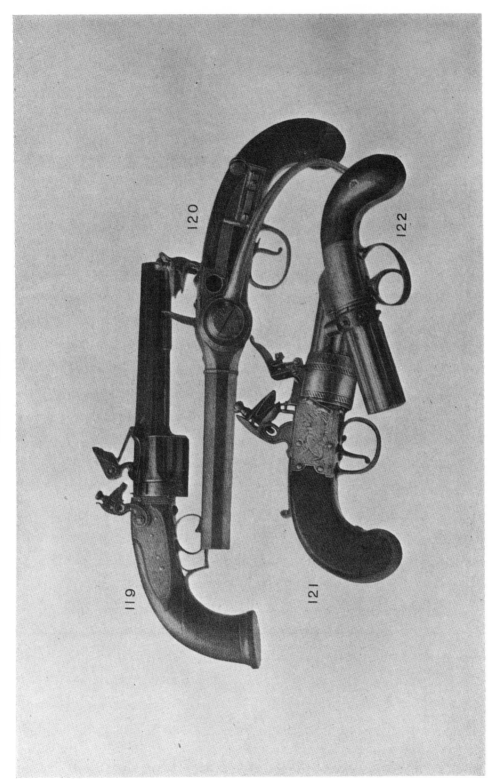

119. Collier Flint Lock Revolver, London, 1818, with Magazine Primer.
120. Repeating Flint Lock Pistol, made for Lord Nelson, by H. W. Mortimer, London, about 1805.

121. Hunter, London. Eighteenth Century "Pepper Pot." A central barrel was connected with one of the six surrounding it, so that the user could begin with a double discharge.
122. Blanch Percussion "Pepper Pot," before 1848.

sufficient compensation for the added weight and danger. They, however, serve to show that the ideal of a rapid repetition of the discharge has been before inventors from almost the earliest period of fire-arms.

The perfecting of the gastight cartridge containing its own means of ignition, was however the necessary factor for the realization in a practical and reliable form of a repeating weapon. The earliest successful repeating rifles were produced in America and were adapted for rim fire (Flobert) ammunition. Revolving chambered weapons had been tried from the earliest times, and in 1850 Colt had perfected his percussion revolving pistol and rifle ; the former, adapted later on for the central fire cartridge, has had world-wide success for the last forty years. In this system, which has been adopted by nearly all revolver makers, both before and since, the chambers are parallel to the axis on which they turn, but other systems have been tried in which the chambers radiated from the axis like the spokes in a wheel, such as the Stephenson-Porter Rifle 1851-4 (group 18, fig. 124). Pistols with a similar arrangement placed horizontally were also made by Cochran as early as 1837, but without success, as there are many obvious objections to it.

The Spencer Rifle was patented in America in 1860 ; it was a very ingenious and original weapon, and was used in the Civil War. It was made at the Harper's Ferry Armoury, at which Mr. Spencer, a civil engineer, held an appointment. The factory itself was captured during the war.

The Spencer Rifle (group 18, fig. 126, and group 19, fig. 133) was very rapid in operation, and held more cartridges, and could be discharged almost as quickly as a revolver, could be reloaded even more quickly, and had not the disadvantage of the break between the chamber and the barrel characteristic of most revolvers.

The difficult problem of obtaining a closed breech and barrel, as in the single breechloading rifle, combined with the rapid repetition of the fire hitherto only associated with the revolver, was successfully achieved for the first time by the Spencer Repeating Rifle.   The cartridges were contained in a tube in the stock, and were fed towards the action by a spring, the semi-circular breech block having both a falling and a rotating motion given to it by the lever forming the trigger guard.   When the block was in its open position a cartridge was projected from the magazine and was held against the face of the block by a spring finger ; the closing of the block by the lever carried the cartridge into the barrel, and the hammer had then to be cocked by the thumb.   The magazine was recharged by removing the tube through a slide in the butt plate.

" In the war (American Civil) this rifle did terrible execution ; at Ball's Bluff one regiment of the Confederates were armed with it, and to them was due the frightful slaughter of that bloody field.

" At Gettysburg, where a part of General Geary's troops were armed with the Spencer, the attack on them by a division of Ewell's (shortly before Stonewall Jackson's) Corps on the night of the 2nd July, was repulsed by a greatly inferior force with terrific destruction of life.   An eye witness said of it, that 'the head of the column, as it was pushed on by those behind, appeared to melt away or sink into the earth, for though continually moving it got no nearer.'

" In the western army the same result followed its use, a regiment armed with it being a match for a division with the ordinary Springfield musket."

Shortly after the invention of this very original and important action, the inevitable competitor appeared, the Henry (American) Repeating Rifle being patented in America in the same year, but does not seem to have been patented in this country, and apparently was not made for long, as the Winchester, patented in America in 1863, very soon completely eclipsed all its rivals. This appears to have been a development of the Henry, as some of the parts are similar.

The first Winchester Rifle, model 1866 (group 18, fig. 128, and group 19, fig. 134), had a tubular magazine under the barrel holding twelve or more .44 calibre rim fire cartridges, according to the length of the barrel and magazine, which were fed to the barrel by a carrier working in a vertical slot or mortice in the action, and operated by a long lever, through a loop in which three fingers were placed when firing or operating the rifle. By means of a "toggle" jointed to the lever, the bolt and firing pin were forced back against the hammer, which was thrust back into the full-cocked position, so that on closing the lever, which pushed a fresh cartridge from the carrier into the barrel, the breech bolt being supported by the "toggle" in its extended position, the trigger could be instantly released.

This rifle could be discharged by an expert at the rate of several shots a second; a brick thrown into the air could be broken in half and one or more of the parts again hit before reaching the ground. A block of wood placed on the ground at a distance of twenty yards or so could be kept dancing about apparently without cessation by a battery of bullets until it was simply a heap of splinters. Two glass balls thrown together from a trap could both be hit before they reached the ground, and many similar feats of rapid aiming and firing which had never before been possible with a single barrelled weapon. Being produced for a very moderate price, of course this marvellous weapon was immediately adopted by the North American Indian, the Cow Boy and Ranchman and Westerner generally throughout America, and in a few years all over the world.   It was partly adopted by the Turkish Army, which had 30,000 of them, and was used, together with the Peabody and the Martini, of which they had 500,000, against the Russians.   Many other systems have been produced in America, based on the same general plan, and operated by a similar lever, also some operated by the left hand, as in the Colt Lightning Rifle, by means of a sliding forepart, first used in the Spencer Gun.   None of these have achieved the popularity of the Winchester, which since 1873 has been made for a central fire cartridge and in a great variety of models.

The enormous success of the Repeating Rifle inevitably attracted the attention of all the military authorities.   The Swiss Army was the first to adopt the repeating principle in 1869 ; their rifle, the Vetterli, fired a copper rim fire cartridge, and was very similar in general construction to the Winchester of 1866, only it was operated by a "door-bolt" instead of a finger lever underneath (group 12, fig. 89).   No other Government followed this example until 1884, when the Mauser, already adopted by Germany, was adapted to the repeating system.   France, having converted the Chassepot to take a gastight metal cartridge a few years previously, in 1886, adopted the Lebel, with which it is still armed.

These three rifles, spoken of as repeaters, all had the cartridges disposed in a tube under the barrel, but in 1888 both Germany and Austria adopted rifles having the box form of magazine, in which the usually five cartridges lie one above another, underneath the bolt, and

GROUP XVIII.

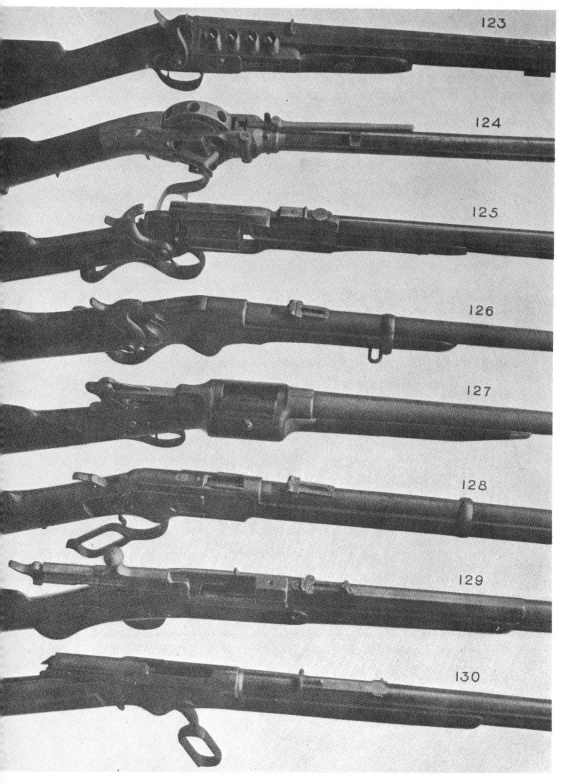

123. MOULD SLIDING LOCK AND FOUR NIPPLES (1825). A SIMILAR
    FLINT LOCK WEAPON WAS MADE BY AITKEN IN 1780.
124. STEPHENSON-PORTER (U.S.A.) (1851-4).
125. COLT (U.S.A.) REVOLVING RIFLE (1850).
126. SPENCER (U.S.A.) REPEATING RIFLE (1860).

127. ROPER (U.S.A.) REPEATING SHOT GUN (1866).
128. WINCHESTER (U.S.A.) REPEATING RIFLE (1873).
129. REMINGTON (U.S.A.) REPEATING RIFLE (1874).
130. MARLIN (U.S.A.) REPEATING RIFLE (1880).

which has now become the general type of military rifle throughout the world.

A further improvement was introduced in these last two rifles by Ferdinand Ritter von Mannlicher, of Steyr, Austria, which has become known as "clip-loading," five cartridges being held together in a spring steel clip, which is placed together with the cartridges right into the magazine, where it is held by a catch, and supported by a narrow spring arm, which passes freely between the sides of the clip and feeds the cartridges up through the clip for the bolt to push them out of the clip and into the barrel (group 20, fig. 143, 144). As the last of the five cartridges is taken from the clip, the clip itself falls to the ground through a hole in the bottom of the magazine (group 20, fig. 143, 144). In the later rifles of both Mannlicher and the equally celebrated inventor, Paul Mauser, of Oberndorf, Germany, the cartridges are held in a narrower spring clip called a "charger," which does not itself enter the magazine, being held in two grooves on the top of the action, but from which the cartridges are stripped by the thumb into the magazine, the charger being removed by hand or thrown out by the bolt on closing the breech (group 20, fig. 145).

I cannot do better than quote from a pamphlet by Mr. R. H. Angier on "Military Small Arms and Ammunition," which was published by my firm in 1902, to give an epitome of the salient points of modern magazine rifles, together with the "Particulars of Rifles," from the same, corrected to date.

"The Magazine Rifle used in the armies of to-day are popularly supposed to be a creation of very recent date. In point of fact, their definite adoption as service arms goes back to 1869, in which year the re-arming of all divisions of the Swiss army with the Vetterli Rifle, was decreed by the Federal Parliament. Most of the Great Powers were experimenting with, or issuing, new models at the time of, or shortly after, the Franco-German War, and there was little difference between the various Rifles finally adopted ; a bolt action gun of 11 m/m (0.433 in.) bore, firing a bullet of about 385 grains with from 1400 to 1450 f.s. at the muzzle, represented the average conditions.   Other arms, at first intended to be substantially more powerful, were finally and reluctantly acknowledged to be failures.   All these Rifles of course used black powder, and were single loaders.   Desultory experiments were made with magazine arms, but no Great Power followed the example of Switzerland until it became known in 1885 that the German Government had quietly re-armed the troops stationed along its Western frontier with repeating Rifles, a modification of their excellent weapon of 1871.

"The inevitable counterstroke soon followed; in the next year, rumours, gradually crystallizing into positive statements, appeared in the public press, of a new Magazine Rifle adopted by the French Government, and being issued with all speed to the French troops.   Everyone will remember the accounts, largely fanciful, given of its wonderful powers, and the precautions, as elaborate as futile, taken by the French Government to preserve the secret of their new ammunition.   The Lebel Rifle was the pioneer of a new era in arms, and of the most marked advance since the introduction of the breechloader.   The essential source of this advance was a new class of propellent, and its effect, a revolution in tactics.

" Externally, the characteristic of the Lebel and succeeding arms, is the greatly increased speed in flight of their projectiles and the low trajectories of the latter ; radical changes both in the ammunition and the arms adapted to its use have brought about this effect.   Black powders, or in general, those which were essentially mechanical mixtures of simple ingredients, have given way to propellents of essentially chemical origin, and the former are now as obsolete for naval or military use, except as bursters for shells, as is muzzleloading artillery.   Rimfire (Vetterli) and rolled sheet (Martini) cartridge shells have disappeared, and bullets have undergone radical modification.

" The essential feature of the new propellents is not their ' smokelessness,' as it is popularly called, but the much higher ballistic efficiency obtained from a given weight ; the small amount of smoke, or vapour, given off by their combustion, is quite an accessory advantage, although one of the utmost tactical value, both for attack and defence.

" High speed of flight was perforce accompanied by a reduction in weight of projectile, in order to keep recoil within reasonable limits.   The benefit of this higher speed could only be secured, at long ranges, by increased sectional density, whence small bores followed as a matter of course. Bullets thus became four or more calibres long, and it soon became apparent that plain lead could not follow the quick twist necessary to give the required longitudinal stability. Thus Major Bode's (of the Swiss Army) invention of 1875, the bullet with hard metal jacket, insuring maximum delivery of energy upon the object attacked, and minimum waste of work spent in deforming the bullet, came into general use, completing the modern military cartridge.

"The chief tactical advantages secured by the new arms are expressed in briefest manner, a large increase of the 'danger zone' at all distances, and the necessity of adequate cover, respectively caused by the flat trajectory and great penetrative powers of the new projectiles. The force of the latter point is best illustrated by the fact that ordinary brick walls are readily breached by modern rifle fire, so that an amount of protection which sufficed in former times is now actually a source of increased danger from the flying fragments caused by present day bullets."

The Magazine Rifle was adopted by the British Government in 1888; the "Lee" action, an American invention, was selected by a committee appointed in 1883, in combination with a "Metford" barrel of .303-inch calibre. In 1895 the Lee-Metford (group 3, fig. 17) was modified in the rifling, and other small changes were embodied, and the rifle was officially entitled the Lee-Enfield. Finally the present pattern of Short Lee-Enfield (group 3, fig. 18 and group 21, fig. 149) was approved in 1903.

The committee appointed in 1883 was empowered to recommend the best magazine action it could find, but the later committee of 1901 was only empowered to suggest such improvements in the Lee-Enfield as they might consider desirable, and were not allowed to consider the adoption of a perfected magazine action and cartridge. Consequently several radical defects, which had escaped the notice of the earlier committee, are present in the later model.

In the first place it must be noted that the original Lee (group 13, fig. 100), made by the Remington Arms Company, was free from some of the defects of its offshoot. It had the same locking lugs on the bolt, behind the magazine, instead of in front as in the Lebel and all later arms, but the stock was in one piece, and therefore the butt could not get loose if exposed to considerable variations of climate, as British rifles must be, all over the world ; and although the action, like the Mauser M/71 and others of similar type, was not symmetrical, it was easy and cheap to machine, and not weakened by the long slot for the "cut-off" in its weakest side, and was of course free from that hideous hump into which the butt is fixed in the British rifle. If it were asked : How could you fix the butt so as to cause the greatest possible bending or twisting strain upon the light action which it is essential should remain true, so as not to interfere with the bearing of the lugs and the shooting of the barrel, let alone the effects of a fall, or the possibility of clubbing the rifle ? the correct answer would be : Put it on exactly as it is done in the British rifle.

It has been rumoured that the origin of the separate butt and forepart in the Lee-Metford was the desire of the authorities to use up a stock of a few thousand short butts, originally prepared for the Martini. If this is so, it has been a very expensive economy, the value of the short butts being about two shillings, for which they could have been easily disposed of, and the additional cost of forging and machining the hump, and fitting the long butt screw, probably add double this to the cost, as it is wasteful alike of metal, time and tools, and the forging has to be about double the weight before machining than would otherwise be required. This has now been repeated in about a million rifles, besides spoiling the design and increasing the weight. In fact, if a separate butt was desired, it could hardly have been designed to embody more disadvantages. Two examples may be mentioned in support of this—the Winchester-Hotchkiss rifle, M/83, and the Lebel M/86. Both have a separate butt, and the action in each case is a thoroughly mechanical adaptation of means

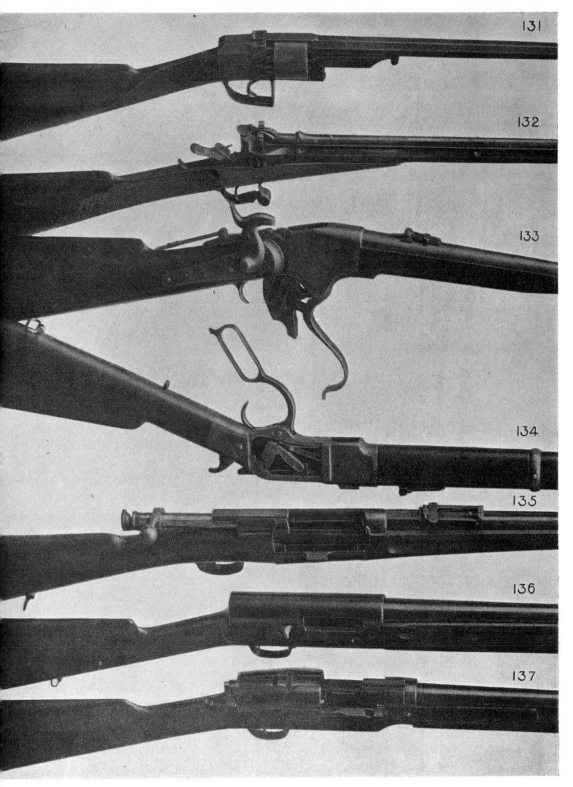

131

132

133

134

135

136

137

HAMMERLESS PERCUSSION REVOLVER.
BELGIAN REPEATING SALOON RIFLE, NEEDLE FIRE.
SPENCER (U.S.A.) REPEATING RIFLE (1860).
WINCHESTER (U.S.A.) REPEATING RIFLE (1863 PATENT, MODEL 1866).

135. SCHULHOF (VIENNA) ROTATING MAGAZINE RIFLE (1886-9).
136. BROWNING (U.S.A.) AUTO-LOADING SHOT GUN (1902).
137. SJÖGREN (SWEDEN) AUTO-LOADING SHOT GUN (1908).

to end, of pleasing shape and free from useless weight. In a bolt such as the Lee, the stress due to the pressure of the cartridge on the front must be borne by the sides of the action connecting the lug bearings with the barrel, but in our rifle the shock from the recoil of the whole arm has also to be transmitted through the action across an abrupt bend to the hump, and so to the butt. In any rationally designed arm the shock from the recoil is transmitted as soon as possible by means of a substantial abutment just under the breech, to the entire shaft of the stock, butt and forepart in one. This is effected in the German M/88 and almost all other European rifles, as well as the Springfield M/03 and M/06, in a manner which leaves nothing to be desired, the abutment under the front end of the action bearing against a substantial steel bolt passing right through the stock from side to side, entirely relieving the action and screws from the shock due to the recoil, and at the same time bracing the stock just in front of the large mortice for the magazine. In our rifle there is such an abutment which is connected to the trigger plate and so to the bottom of the hump, but this does not prevent the action as the more rigid member of the girder so formed carrying most of the shock.

In a vertical box magazine there is always a difficulty, when using rimmed cartridges, in preventing the rim of the upper cartridge when placed in the magazine, from getting behind the rim of the under one. In the Lee magazine, patented in 1879, a zig-zag spring was used, but afterwards a double C spring was substituted under the platform, and in the Lee-Metford the platform wobbled on the end of a C spring by means of a pivot in two guides, admitting of depressing the cartridge too much at the front end when loading, and accidentally placing another with its rim behind the rim of the lower one, thus causing a complete jam, as the top cartridge cannot be pushed into the barrel, which takes a lot of fiddling about to adjust, and of course is most likely to occur at a critical moment.   In its later forms the magazine has been slightly improved, but the only radical cure is the adoption of a grooved or rimless cartridge, which is obviously necessary if one cartridge is to slide over another in a vertical magazine, and would render the whole arrangement fool-proof.

A glance at the fore-part when detached from the rifle is sufficient to show that the design has been altered, as no one capable of designing the original model would have consented to cut off the fore-part so close to the trigger hole that the section of wood left to hold the two sides together is not much more than the area of a lead pencil, and the sides are therefore braced together with a steel staple kept in place by a brass pin, so that although new, it looks like a piece of mended furniture.   In the latest production of our Small Arms Committee, the short Lee-Enfield 1903, an unpardonable fault has been committed in the retention of the backwardly-placed locking lugs of the original Lee.   Since 1886 all high-class military rifles have had symmetrical forwardly placed lugs interlocking in corresponding grooves cut in the action at the front.   This is the simplest and strongest form of breech closure at present known for military rifles. Taking up the thrust of the gas pressure as closely as possible to its point of production, it relieves the remainder of the action from all stress due to this cause ; to appreciate the effect of rational as opposed to irrational design in this particular, it is sufficient to compare the Lee-Enfield action with that of a Mauser or a Mannlicher. Although so much lighter than that of the Lee-Enfield, a Mauser action requires a gas pressure of over 7000 atmospheres to produce rupture, two-thirds of this pressure at most being required to disable the British action and possibly the user also. Why was not the central forward locking adopted in 1889? The talented Mannlicher used this system in one of his models in 1878, and in 1886 the Lebel proclaimed its superiority in the most striking manner. Even admitting, against all reason, that the superiority of central forward locking was "not proven" in 1889, no possible excuse can palliate the blunder of 1903. It has been rumoured that when the committee was appointed, they were specifically instructed "not to meddle with the bolt," but one is naturally loth to believe such a statement, especially as the weakness of the bolt and action had been notorious from its first adoption, and the rifles were only subjected to a very inadequate margin of strain at the proof in consequence ; moreover, the original makers of the Lee Rifle, the Remington Arms Co., had in 1898 improved their own model by moving the lugs to a forward position on the bolt. There seems only one small difficulty in the alteration, which every rifle expert in the country wishes to see made, and that is—if it is not desirable, for purely financial reasons, to alter the form of the cartridge—that in pushing a rimmed cartridge into the barrel, the rim would have to pass the groove in the action which forms the bearing for the locking lugs, and in passing might trip against the front edge of the groove, but this is prevented in the Lebel, Russian and other rifles by bevelling the forward edge of the recess for the locking lugs, so as to form a funnel-shaped slope leading to the mouth of the chamber.

Even the shooting is affected by the position of the lugs. All metal such as is used in rifle actions will elongate under stress, and the sides being unequal they elongate unequally, allowing both bolt and barrel to depart from their true axis, and producing a noticeable effect in the sighting of the arm and a wholly gratuitous difficulty in the calculation of trajectory tables.

One of the real improvements in the 1903 rifle was the robust and well made back sight, on the cam system, the slide of which was adjusted by an easy and natural squeeze between the thumb and finger as in the German Mauser 1898, which does not disturb the poise of the rifle in the hands.   But in the latest Mark 3 model, an alteration has been approved which is likely to prove quite un-workable, and let us hope will be abandoned on the first opportunity. In order to release the slide it is now necessary to press a spring stud on the left side only, to allow a worm gear to disengage from the half section of a female screw cut in the side of the tangent.   With the intention of enabling the worm to be turned by the fingers, it is cross cut at about right angles to the thread, so that it has the ap-pearance of coarse knurling, and makes it act as a scratch brush or blunt milling cutter, but, unlike the worm in the proverb, this worm will not turn, unless released by pressing again on the stud, which nullifies the fine adjustment intended.   After handling the German Mauser, 1898, and realising the absolute facility with which the sight can be adjusted, such an unwarworthy arrangement as the worm gear sight of the Mark 3 rifle makes one writhe with vexation.   It may be foolish to retain the auxiliary dial sight, but at least it is harmless—you need not use it—but this worm gear will fool the soldier every time the sight is adjusted.   The full significance of facility in handling seems incomprehensible to many people.

But what is the purpose of these refinements?   Naturally, their designers say, to enable the soldier to get the full advantage of the

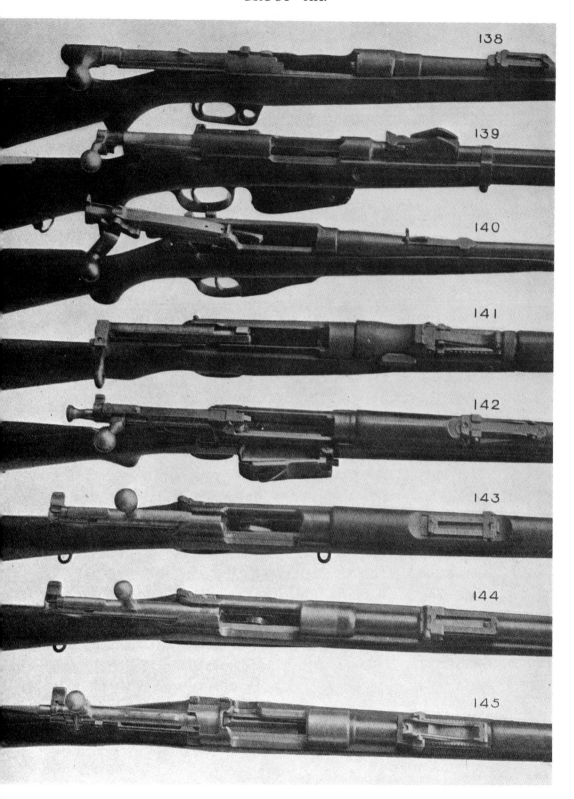

138

139

140

141

142

143

144

145

UR STRAIGHT-PULL-BOLT MAGAZINE RIFLES.

138. KRNKA (1887-9).
139. MANNLICHER (1886).
140. LEE, U.S. NAVY (1893-5).
141. ROSS, CANADA (1905).

FOUR DOOR-BOLT MAGAZINE RIFLES.

142. KRAG-JORGENSEN, NORWAY, DENMARK, AND U.S.A. (1889).
143. MANNLICHER, ROUMANIAN (1886).
144. GERMAN, MAUSER AND COMMISSION, MANNLICHER SYSTEM (1888).
145. GERMAN MAUSER (1898).

accuracy of his arm, always with the ideal of an army of sharp-shooters, each capable of picking off single men at 1000 yards with every shot. Impossible! because war is not sport, because men have nerves and the target shoots back, because no convenient flags and other range accessories are found on the battle field, and above all, because of the inevitable inaccuracy in estimating ranges, and it can be said, without exaggeration, that nine-tenths of the effect of infantry fire depends on range estimation, and less than one-tenth on the extreme accuracy of the rifle and its accessories. This is considered an elementary truth by the recognised tacticians on the continent.

For the few men who master the art of shooting at long target or medium battle ranges, a very different sighting appliance is required, namely an aperture close to the eye, but the addition of complications to the rifle sights of the mass as a means of overcoming the errors of range estimation is not justified by practical musketry considerations.

A welcome improvement, adopted from continental practice, is the drag-pull trigger, this divides its action into two parts, the first a long but easy drag, which nearly lifts the sear out of its engagement, and a short but much harder final release, which allows a very steady "let-off."

Taking the Lee-Enfield as a whole, it may be confidently asserted that no gunsmith, worthy of the name, would have passed such a design. It is said that "they do these things better in France," and we might add Germany, Austria, Switzerland, United States of America, Russia, Japan, and most other countries.

All recent experience has shown that the rifle is still by far the most deadly weapon that is put into the hands of an army, in spite of automatic machine guns and quick-firing artillery with high explosive shells.

———

Re-enter FALSTAFF AND THE JUSTICES.

FALSTAFF—Come, sir, which men shall I have?

SHALLOW—Four of which you please.

BARDOLPH—Sir, a word with you : I have three pound to free Mouldy and Bullcalf.

FALSTAFF—Go to ; well.

SHALLOW—Come, Sir John, which four will you have ?

FALSTAFF—Do you choose for me.

SHALLOW—Marry, then, Mouldy, Bullcalf, Feeble, and Shadow.

FALSTAFF—Mouldy and Bullcalf ; for you Mouldy, stay at home till you are past service : and for your part, Bullcalf, grow till you come unto it.

SHALLOW—Sir John, Sir John, do not yourself wrong ! they are your likeliest men, and I would have you served with the best.

FALSTAFF—Will you tell me, Master Shallow, how to choose a man ? Care I for the limb, the thewes, the stature, bulk, and big assemblance of a man ! Give me the spirit, Master Shallow. Here's Wart ; you see what a ragged appearance it is : a' shall charge you and discharge you with the motion of a pewterer's hammer, come off and on swifter than he that gibbets on the brewer's bucket. And this same half-faced fellow, Shadow ; give me this man : he presents no mark to the enemy ; the foemen may with as great aim level at the edge of a penknife. And for a retreat ; how swiftly will this Feeble the woman's tailor run off ! O, give me the spare men, and spare me the great ones. Put me a caliver into Wart's hand Bardolph.

BARDOLPH—Hold, Wart, traverse ; thus, thus thus.

FALSTAFF—Come, manage me your caliver. So : very well : go to : very good, exceeding good. O, give me always a little, lean, old, chapt, bald shot. Well said, i' faith, Wart ; thou'rt a good scab : hold, there's a tester for thee.

Henry IV., Second Part, Act III., Sc. II.

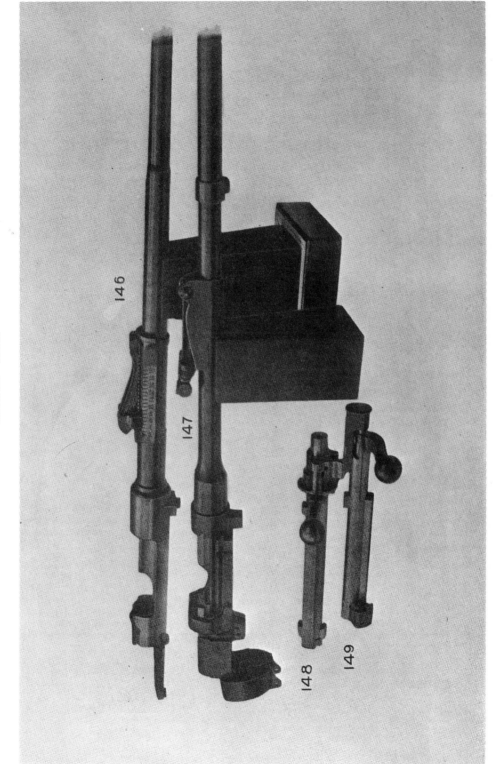

GROUP XXI.

146. MAUSER ACTION (1898).
147. LEE-ENFIELD ACTION (1903).

148. MAUSER BOLT, TWO FORWARD AND ONE REAR LOCKING LUGS.
149. LEE-ENFIELD BOLT, TWO REAR LOCKING LUGS.

APPENDIX.

TABLE I.—PARTICULARS OF MILITARY MAGAZINE RIFLES.

Country.	Date.	Name of Rifle.	Calibre.		Muzzle Velocity.		Muzzle Energy.		Recoil.		Weight of Bullet.		Danger Zone.*	
			mm.	in.	m/s	ft/s.	mkg.	ft. lbs.	mkg.	ft. lbs.	grams.	grains.	m.	yds.
France ...	1886-93[1]	Lebel	8·00	·315	632	2073	306	2211	1·31	9·5	15·00	232	537	587
Austria ...	1888-90	Mannlicher ...	8·00	·315	620	2034	310	2240	1·29	9·3	15·80	244	530	579
Austria ...	1895	Mannlicher ...	8·00	·315	620	2034	310	2240	1·59	11·5	15·80	244	530	579
Denmark ...	1889[2]	Krag-Jörgensen	8·00	·315	625	2050	306	2211	1·28	9·2	15·40	238	511	558
Germany ...	1888	Mannlicher ...	7·90	·311	640	2100	307	2218	1·43	10·3	14·70	227	534	584
Germany ...	1898-02[3]	Mauser ...	7·90	·311	880	2885	395	2854	1·30	9·4	10·00	154	690	754
Britain ...	1888[2]-95	Lee	7·70	·303	630	2065	281	2030	1·07	7·7	13·90	215	530	579
Britain ...	1903	Lee	7·70	·303	610	2000	264	1908	1·11	8·0	13·90	215	514	562
Belgium ...	1889	Mauser ...	7·65	·301	600	1968	259	1871	1·05	7·6	14·10	218	528	577
Turkey ...	1890	Mauser ...	7·65	·301	652	2138	297	2147	1·25	9·0	13·70	212	528	577
Russia ...	1891	Mossin	7·62	·300	620	2034	267	1928	1·05	7·6	13·60	210	520	568
U.S.A. ...	1892-98	Krag-Jörgensen...	7·62	·300	610	2000	269	1945	1·18	8·5	14·25	220	513	561
U.S.A. ...	1895[5]	Lee Straight-pull...	6·00	·236	777	2550	224	1620	0·56	4·1	7·28	112	563	615
U.S.A. ...	1903-06[3] [6]	New Springfield...	7·62	·300	825	2700	336	2427	1·14	8·2	9·70	150	661	723
Switzerland	1889-96[4]	Schmidt-Rubin ...	7·50	·295	610	2000	262	1893	0·89	6·4	13·80	213	519	567
Switzerland	1900	Short Rifle ...	7·50	·295	591	1937	246	1777	1·02	7·4	13·80	213	—	—
Spain	1893	Mauser	7·00	·276	710	2328	288	2082	0·99	7·2	11·20	173	573	626
Italy	1891	Parravicini-Carcano	6·50	·256	700	2295	263	1900	0·91	6·6	10·50	162	558	610
Roumania...	1893	Mannlicher ...	6·50	·256	740	2427	289	2088	0·96	6·9	10·33	160	573	626
Norway ...	1894	Krag-Jörgensen ...	6·50	·256	730	2396	274	1980	0·87	6·3	10·10	156	601	657
Holland ...	1895	Mannlicher ...	6·50	·256	745	2443	289	2088	0·85	6·1	10·20	158	560	612
Sweden ...	1896	Mauser	6·50	·256	730	2396	274	1980	0·87	6·3	10·10	156	605	661
Japan	1897[2]	Arisaka	6·50	·256	730	2396	286	2066	0·93	6·7	10·50	162	600	655
—	1904-07	Mauser	7·90	·311	810	2657	440	3178	1·79	12·9	13·15	203	691	755
—	1904-07	Mauser	7·65	·301	830	2723	415	2996	1·55	11·2	11·82	183	703	768
—	1904-07	Mauser	7·00	·276	895	2935	408	2946	1·39	10·0	10·00	154	771	842
—	1904-07	Mauser	6·50	·256	900	2950	374	2700	1·26	9·1	9·07	140	799	873

1. The French Rifle now fires a solid copper alloy bullet ("balle D"), weight, 12·8 grams; muzzle velocity, about 2700 ft/s.
2. Metford shape of grooves.
3. "S" Bullet ("Spitz geschoss"), weight, 10·0 grams, German; 9·7 grams, U.S.

4. "S" Bullet, adopted end of 1908, sensibly same ballistics as German.
5. Since abandoned.
6. The New Springfield has all the essential features of the Mauser.

* Range at which the summit of trajectory is exactly the average height of a man, 1·70 m = 66·9 in. above the line of sight.

NOTE.—Equivalent English dimensions of Foreign Rifles are approximate.

TABLE II.—PARTICULARS OF MILITARY MAGAZINE RIFLES.

Country	Date	Name of Rifle	No. of Grooves	Width of Grooves mm.	Width of Grooves in.	Depth of Grooves mm.	Depth of Grooves in.	Pitch mm	Pitch in.	Length of Barrel mm.	Length of Barrel in.	Length of Rifle m.	Length of Rifle in.	Weight of Rifle kg.	Weight of Rifle lbs.
France	1886-93	Lebel	4	4·20	·165	·150	·0059	240	9·45	800	31·50	1·307	51·7	4·18	9·21
Austria	1888-90	Mannlicher	4	4·20	·165	·200	·0079	250	9·84	765	30·10	1·281	50·4	4·45	9·82
Austria	1895	Mannlicher	4	4·20	·165	·200	·0079	250	9·84	765	30·10	1·272	50·1	3·65	8·05
Denmark	1889	Krag-Jörgensen	6	3·00	·118	·140	·0055	300	11·80	836	33·00	1·330	52·4	4·25	9·37
Germany	1888	Mannlicher	4	4·40	·173	·150	·0060	240	9·45	740	29·10	1·245	49·0	3·80	8·38
Germany	1898-02	Mauser	4	4·40	·173	·150	·0060	240	9·45	740	29·10	1·250	49·2	4·15	9·16
Britain	1888-95	Lee	5	2·42	·095	·127	·0050	254	10·00	767	30·20	1·257	49·5	4·20	9·26
Britain	1903	Lee	5	2·42	·095	·127	·0050	254	10·00	640	25·20	1·130	44·5	3·75	8·27
Belgium	1889	Mauser	4	4·45	·175	·170	·0067	—	—	779	30·70	1·277	50·3	3·90	8·60
Turkey	1890	Mauser	4	4·20	·165	·125	·0049	250	9·84	740	29·10	1·235	48·6	3·90	8·60
Russia	1891	Mossin	4	3·99	·157	·150	·0059	240	9·45	800	31·50	1·288	50·7	3·99	8·80
U.S.A.	1892-98	Krag-Jörgensen	4	4·47	·176	·100	·0040	254	10·00	762	30·00	1·247	49·1	3·97	8·75
U.S.A.	1895	Lee Straight-pull	6	2·54	·100	·102	·0040	165	6·50	711	28·00	1·209	47·6	3·86	8·50
U.S.A.	1903-06	New Springfield	4	4·47	·176	·100	·0040	254	10·00	610	24·00	1·098	43·2	3·95	8·70
Switzerland	1889-96	Schmidt-Rubin	3	3·93	·155	·100	·0040	270	10·60	780	30·70	1·302	51·3	4·65	10·25
Switzerland	1900	Short Rifle	3	3·93	·155	·100	·0040	270	10·60	593	23·35	1·100	43·3	3·85	8·49
Spain	1893	Mauser	4	3·90	·154	·125	·0049	220	8·67	738	29·00	1·235	48·6	3·90	8·60
Italy	1891	Parravicini-Carcano	4	3·10	·122	·130	·0051	200	7·87	780	30·70	1·290	50·8	3·80	8·38
Roumania	1893	Mannlicher	4	2·55	·100	·150	·0059	200	7·87	725	28·60	1·229	48·4	4·00	8·81
Norway	1894	Krag-Jörgensen	4	3·00	·118	·150	·0059	200	7·87	762	30·00	1·260	49·6	4·00	8·81
Holland	1895	Mannlicher	4	2·55	·100	·150	·0059	200	7·87	799	31·10	1·287	50·7	4·30	9·48
Sweden	1896	Mauser	4	2·55	·100	·150	·0059	200	7·87	738	29·00	1·260	49·6	3·92	8·65
Japan	1897	Arisaka	6	2·90	·114	·150	·0059	200	7·87	790	31·10	1·270	50·0	3·90	8·60
—	1904-07	Mauser	4	4·40	·173	·150	·0059	240	9·45	740	29·10	1·250	49·2	4·10	9·04
—	1904-07	Mauser	4	4·20	·165	·125	·0049	250	9·84	740	29·10	1·250	49·2	4·10	9·04
—	1904-07	Mauser	4	3·90	·154	·125	·0049	220	8·67	740	29·10	1·250	49·2	4·00	8·81
—	1904-07	Mauser	4	2·55	·100	·125	·0049	200	7·87	740	29·10	1·250	49·2	3·75	8·27

MILITARY RIFLE CARTRIDGES.

FRANCE.—8 M/M LEBEL, M/86—93.

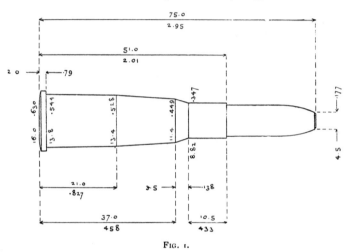

FIG. 1.

SUPERPOSED LEBEL CARTRIDGES.

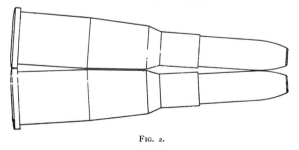

FIG. 2.

AUSTRIA.—8 m/m MANNLICHER, M/90—95.

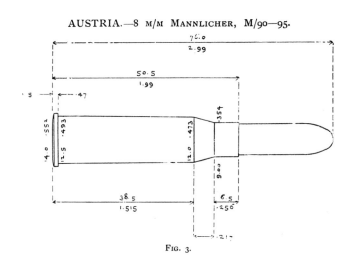

FIG. 3.

DENMARK.—8 m/m KRAG-JÖRGENSEN, M/89.

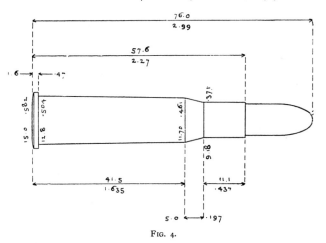

FIG. 4.

GERMANY.—7.9 M/M M/88 AND M/98.

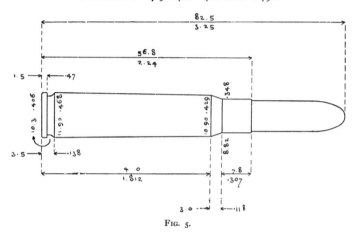

FIG. 5.

GREAT BRITAIN.— 303 LEE, M/89.

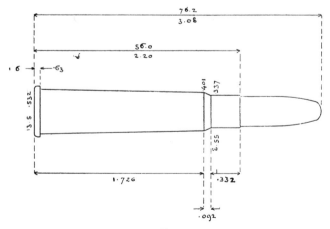

FIG. 6.

TURKEY.—7.65 M/M Mauser, M/90.

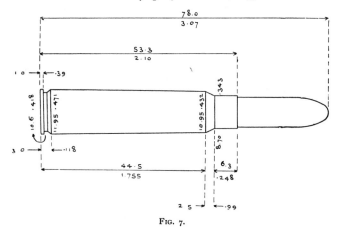

Fig. 7.

RUSSIA.—7.62 M/M Mossin, M/91.

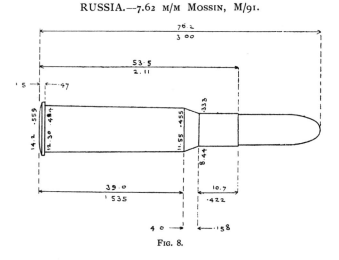

Fig. 8.

UNITED STATES.—300 KRAG-JÖRGENSEN, M/92—96.

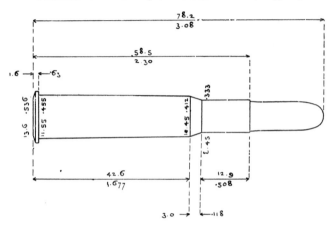

FIG. 9.

SWITZERLAND.—7.5 M/M SCHMIDT-RUBIN, M/89—96.

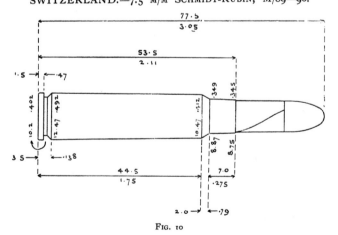

FIG. 10

SPAIN.—7 M/M MAUSER, M/93—95.

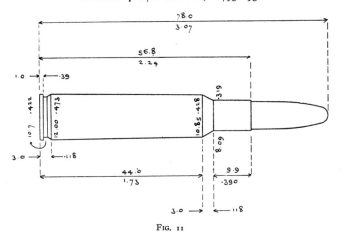

FIG. 11

SWEDEN.—6.5 M/M MAUSER, M/96.

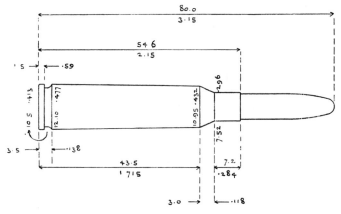

FIG. 12.

ITALY.—6.5 M/M Parravicini-Carcano, M/91.

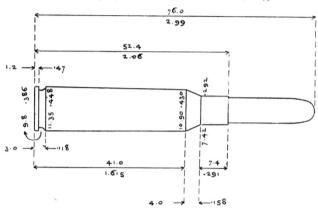

Fig. 13.

ROUMANIA.—6.5 M/M Mannlicher, M/93.

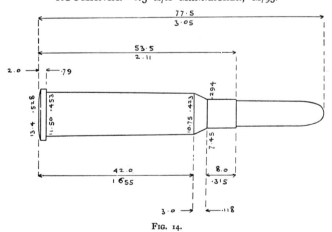

Fig. 14.

6.5 M/M MANNLICHER-SCHONAUER, M/1900.

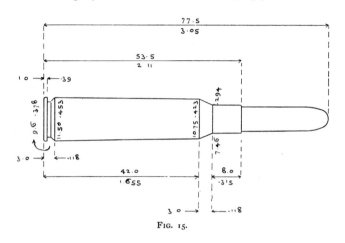

FIG. 15.

6 M/M LEE STRAIGHT-PULL, M/95.

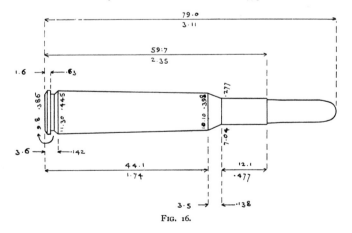

FIG. 16.

INDEX.

INDEX.

INDEX.

INDEX.

INDEX.